# Design Thinking

Design Thinking is a set of strategic and creative processes and principles used in the planning and creation of products and solutions to human-centered design problems.

With design and innovation being two key driving principles, this series focuses on, but is not limited to, the following areas and topics:

- User Interface (UI) and User Experience (UX) Design
- Psychology of Design
- Human-Computer Interaction (HCI)
- Ergonomic Design
- Product Development and Management
- Virtual and Mixed Reality (VR/XR)
- User-Centered Built Environments and Smart Homes
- Accessibility, Sustainability and Environmental Design
- Learning and Instructional Design
- Strategy and best practices

This series publishes books aimed at designers, developers, storytellers and problem-solvers in industry to help them understand current developments and best practices at the cutting edge of creativity, to invent new paradigms and solutions, and challenge Creatives to push boundaries to design bigger and better than before.

More information about this series at https://link.springer.com/bookseries/15933.

# Generative Art with JavaScript and SVG

## Utilizing Scalable Vector Graphics and Algorithms for Creative Coding and Design

David Matthew

Apress®

*Generative Art with JavaScript and SVG: Utilizing Scalable Vector Graphics and Algorithms for Creative Coding and Design*

David Matthew
Limerick, Ireland

ISBN-13 (pbk): 979-8-8688-0085-6          ISBN-13 (electronic): 979-8-8688-0086-3
https://doi.org/10.1007/979-8-8688-0086-3

Managing Director, Apress Media LLC: Welmoed Spahr
Acquisitions Editor: James Robinson-Prior
Development Editor: Jim Markham
Editorial Assistant: Gryffin Winkler

Cover designed by Isaac Soler at eStudioCalamar and David Matthew

Distributed to the book trade worldwide by Springer Science+Business Media New York, 1 New York Plaza, 1 FDR Dr, New York, NY 10004. Phone 1-800-SPRINGER, fax (201) 348-4505, e-mail orders-ny@springer-sbm.com, or visit www.springeronline.com. Apress Media, LLC is a California LLC and the sole member (owner) is Springer Science + Business Media Finance Inc (SSBM Finance Inc). SSBM Finance Inc is a **Delaware** corporation.

For information on translations, please e-mail booktranslations@springernature.com; for reprint, paperback, or audio rights, please e-mail bookpermissions@springernature.com.

Apress titles may be purchased in bulk for academic, corporate, or promotional use. eBook versions and licenses are also available for most titles. For more information, reference our Print and eBook Bulk Sales web page at http://www.apress.com/bulk-sales.

Any source code or other supplementary material referenced by the author in this book is available to readers on the Github repository. For more detailed information, please visit https://www.apress.com/gp/services/source-code.

Paper in this product is recyclable

*Dedicated to the deeply human experience of creating art.*

# Table of Contents

# About the Author

**David Matthew** is a web developer, designer and musician who is passionate about the intersection of art, music, and computer science.

He writes about creative coding, generative art, music visualization and other related themes on his website davidmatthew.ie. He is also a regular producer of generative art and shares his work on Instagram (@davidmatthew_ie).

# About the Technical Reviewer

 **Eoin Ó. Conchúir**, PhD, is the founder of Bitesize Irish for Irish language learners. His art can be found on vibrantconflux.com.

# Acknowledgments

I want to thank first those who should always come first: my incredible wife Sandra, my beautiful boy Noah, my constant companion Kow, and my amazing mum, who has always believed in me.

Thank you to my technical reviewer Eoin Ó Conchúir, whose expertise and rigorous code checking weeded out many an error and prompted further clarity on points I had left overly vague. Your contribution means a better book overall, and any remaining errors are mine alone.

Thank you to my editing team at Apress: James Robinson Prior, Gryffin Winkler, and James Markham. In the 15 months since embarking on this project, I've moved house, changed jobs, and, most life-changing of all, welcomed a newborn into my life. Amidst all this change (and sometimes chaos), you've remained exceptionally understanding, flexible, and enthusiastic.

In the broader generative art and creative coding community, I'd like to thank some notable individuals who have inspired my own work and continue to amaze me with their generosity and ingenuity: Pablo Almunia, whose excellent gySVG library was the inspiration behind SvJs and who provided invaluable insights for the first chapter; Ahmad Moussa (a.k.a. Gorilla Sun) whose writing keeps so many of us artists in the loop; Sara Soueidan, whose pioneering work on SVG filters I always find myself returning to; Matt Pearson, one of the first authors to ignite in me that generative spark; Keith Peters, for helping me and many other coders be less afraid of math; and Dan Shiffman, the genius behind the classic work The Nature of Code, and whose enthusiasm is so infectious I can't quite capture it in words (go watch his YouTube videos under the moniker The Coding Train to see what I mean).

## ACKNOWLEDGMENTS

Finally, thank you to my friends and family for all the support. Daire, for your sense of humour (and pretending to NFT anything I post to Instagram); Stephen (founder of letsfundit.ie, a charity well worth a plug) for the office craic and always asking how the book was going. Steven S, for getting me through tough times. To my new team at UL, thank you for being so welcoming and all-round amazing. And to my siblings Brian, Paul, Claire and Sarah, thanks for promising to read this book cover to cover (just joking - but you need to at least read the back!).

# Introduction

A caveat before we begin: generative art, and creative coding more generally, can become an all-consuming addiction. "Just one more iteration" is a refrain you might hear from those unfortunate artists caught in its thrall. Creatives craving that next generative hit mixed with just the right amount of randomness.

The purpose of this book is to deal out this computational devilry in small doses, in a clear, logical fashion, so you can approach this topic safely and with your sanity intact. We will encounter organic forms borne of mechanical precision, unpredictable swathes of color cover our screens, lines and shapes flocking together in impossible harmony, and see complex structures emerge from simple rules. This is the essence of generative art, where not all is in your control.

That said, it's a medium that requires time, patience, and skill on the part of the artist – no less so than with other artistic mediums. And although I might be exaggerating the power it has over its practitioners, the point I really want to make is that coding has this expressive side to it – it can be frustrating and headache-inducing, sure – but it can also fascinate and inspire. If I can equip you with some new generative tools and techniques, and in the process excite you just a little about their creative possibilities – possibilities that extend beyond the field of art into those of design and web development – this book will have more than done its job.

# What You Should Know

As a reader, what should you know before tackling this book? It will no doubt be easier if you are comfortable with the core concepts of programming, like variables, functions, loops, and conditionals. These kinds of concepts carry over from language to language, differing mainly with respect to syntax, so if you come from a language other than JavaScript, then that's completely fine.

If you have no prior programming experience, we will be covering the concepts required in Chapter 2, but I should emphasize that this book is not intended to be an introduction to programming. The second chapter is best thought of as a primer, a jumping-off point for a deeper dive elsewhere. A short introductory course would really benefit you here. Personally I'd recommend the wonderful freeCodeCamp.com, a site I've spent many hours using myself. It offers free interactive tutorials on the basics of HTML, CSS, and JavaScript, and much more besides.

For those coming from another language, like Python, PHP, or C#, the second chapter may still be valuable, to be sure you're acquainted with the syntax and some of the idiosyncrasies of JavaScript.

If you're already a practicing web developer, you could skip (or quickly skim) Chapter 2, depending on your level of experience. If you're unfamiliar with any of the techniques or syntax used in our opening example (which we'll end Chapter 1 with), I'd encourage you to give the second chapter a read, where they'll be fully explained. The field of web development is vast enough that what is bread and butter to one developer might be bleeding edge to another.

# What You Will Learn

I mentioned previously that I'll be equipping you with some new tools and techniques. Let's flesh these out.

# Tools

On the tool end of things, we'll be using the following:

- JavaScript and the SvJs library. I'll elaborate on this further later.

- A code editor. Here I'll be giving you a choice between

  - Visual Studio Code (an excellent open source code editor)

  - CodePen (a popular online code editor)

- If you opt to use Visual Studio Code (which I recommend), we'll also be using Node.js and NPM to manage dependencies (a good habit to get into as a developer).

All code examples are available on both GitHub and CodePen, so feel free to follow along whichever way you prefer. You can of course do both, work locally with a code editor but check out CodePen examples online for quick inspiration. For convenience, I'll organize and embed all CodePen examples at davidmatthew.ie/generative-art-javascript-svg.

# Techniques

In terms of the techniques we'll tackle, by the end of this book, you should have a good overview of the following:

- The main functionality of the SvJs library and how it relates to the SVG spec

- Creating generative art sketches with JavaScript using ES6+ syntax

- Generating primitive SVG shapes

- Creating iterative variations of sketches by randomizing parameters

- Using noise to create organic variance

- Generating complex SVG paths

- Making sketches interactive

- Animating sketches

- Using SVG filters generatively

We'll be covering a lot of ground, so don't put yourself under pressure to understand everything. I must have encountered certain programming concepts umpteen times before the proverbial penny finally dropped (JavaScript promises anyone?), and whenever understanding did finally dawn, it would usually be because I was experimenting with something I *wanted* to build, rather than repeating tutorial steps by rote. Tutorials and instructional books certainly have their place (I wouldn't be writing this book otherwise), but it's important that you take what *you* want from them, rather than seeing them as syllabi to be strictly followed.

A sense of play is important, particularly when it comes to art. And although I mentioned tools previously, I would prefer if you viewed this book as more of a toybox than a toolbox. When I think of tools, I think of problems that need fixing, like the loose hinges on that crooked cabinet you're going to tighten any day now. Tools tend to be more functional than fun, and I'd like you to have some fun with this book.

# CHAPTER 1

# The Beginner's Path

Before journeying along any path, the groundwork needs to be in place.
In this opening chapter, that's what we'll do, lay the groundwork. We'll
introduce SVG, explain what makes it a uniquely powerful image format,
and show how it can be used with JavaScript to create generative art. In the
process, we'll set up our tools and a template we can use for subsequent
sketches.

## Why JavaScript and SvJs?

Most books about generative art use a Java-based language called
Processing, or its JavaScript port p5.js. Processing was created specifically
for artists and designers new to coding and has a large and active
community. So why doesn't this book use it?

My first forays into generative art were with Processing, so I certainly
acknowledge its value. I quickly moved to p5.js when the library was first
released in 2013, which allowed generative sketches to be written directly
in JavaScript, the language of the Web. But when I wanted to integrate
some of my own sketches into real-world web development projects, its
limitations quickly showed. It's a *large* library, clocking in at close to a
megabyte at last check, and while that may not sound like much, it's a lot
by web development standards.

© David Matthew 2024
D. Matthew, *Generative Art with JavaScript and SVG*, Design Thinking,
https://doi.org/10.1007/979-8-8688-0086-3_1

The p5.js library is built on top of the HTML Canvas API, which I soon discovered is actually quite straightforward to use. Using this API directly, I was able to achieve much the same results as with p5.js, so that became my go-to. However, the output of all my sketches – p5.js or Canvas – was still resolution-dependent bitmap graphics, devoid of any semantic content. What does that mean, and why does it matter (to me at least)? Let me explain.

# Introducing Scalable Vector Graphics

Back in the early days of the Web, when dial-up modems were dominant and connecting to the Internet was anything but instant, bandwidth came at a premium. File sizes had to be super small if you wanted a page to load in your lifetime, and bitmap images, such as JPGs and PNGs, were the main bandwidth bottleneck.

Bitmap images – also known as raster images – are comprised of large chunks of data (or bits), and generally speaking, if you want a larger image, you need more bits, which means a bigger file size. SVG, on the other hand, is a vector format, which is fundamentally different. SVG can be scaled to any dimension, all without a corresponding increase in file size, and it is always dazzlingly sharp and crisp. This is possible because it doesn't bother itself with the bits (i.e., pixels) needed to paint the image to the screen, but rather describes the image to be rendered at a more abstract, semantic level. And it does this in much the same way that HTML describes the structure and content of a web page. As the Mozilla Developer Network puts it

---

SVG is, essentially, to graphics what HTML is to text.

---

The SVG format was not only a powerful solution to a practical bandwidth problem; it was a nonproprietary format officially standardized by the World Wide Web Consortium (which is as good as future-proofing gets in the world of web technology). The stage was set for its adoption as far back as 1999, but unfortunately browser vendors dragged their feet and were extremely slow to introduce support. So for the longest time (in Internet terms at least), SVG languished in obscurity. It only really got the support it deserved with the decline of Flash (Adobe's proprietary format that required a plug-in to run and was often riddled with security vulnerabilities) and the rise of responsive design and retina (or high PPI) screens, where its scalability and sharpness really shine.

These days we can use the format freely without worry, but to use it for the odd icon and logo is one thing; to tap its full potential is another.

## Native SVG

As SVG is a declarative language like HTML, it's very human-readable and easy to get started with. Just like HTML elements, SVG elements are written using opening and closing angle brackets and contain attributes with values. Here, for example, is how you'd create a circle:

```
<circle r="125" cy="250" cx="250" fill="cyan"/>
```

The attributes r, cx, cy, and fill in the preceding example refer to the circle's radius, the x and y coordinates of its center, and the color to fill it with. All are sensibly named and simple to follow.

Some SVG elements will contain other elements nested within them, referred to as their child nodes or children, and will therefore need opening and closing tags. One prominent example is the parent <svg> element itself, which contains all other SVG elements.

As an example of how you might handwrite an SVG, here is the markup underlying a very simple composition in the style of Hilma af Klint, arguably the first abstract artist in Western art history.

```
<svg width="500" height="500" style="background-color:
#ad3622">
  <title>A simple Hilma af Klint-inspired knock-off</title>
  <circle r="125" cy="250" cx="250" fill="#d0d1c9"/>
  <circle r="100" cy="250" cx="250" fill="#1c1c1c"/>
  <circle r="75" cy="250" cx="250" fill="#5085b4"/>
  <circle r="50" cy="250" cx="250" fill="#d6a946"/>
</svg>
```

As you can see, SVG is written in such a way as to preserve the semantics of the code. Search engines love this; no longer are they looking at an impenetrable wall of pixels; they can clearly see the *intent* within the markup. In this case, four circles displayed in the order they're written, with a title for extra accessibility. Figure 1-1 shows how this markup appears when rendered.

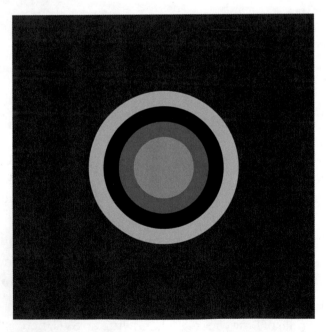

***Figure 1-1.*** *A simple composition in the style of Hilma af Klint's Svanen (The Swan)*

Declarative formats are straightforward to read, but their weakness is that they can become tedious to write. What if we wanted 100 circles instead of four? With native SVG, we'd have to handwrite all of them, one after the other. And if we wanted to display our circles at random cx and cy positions, each with a randomly selected fill, this isn't possible at all. Variables, loops, functions, and all the fun stuff of imperative programming aren't available to us. Declarative formats are concerned more with the *what* of a program rather than the *how*. The how, however, will very much matter to us. Without the how, we wouldn't have algorithms, and algorithms are essential to generative art.

Algorithms are like recipes; they contain the steps you need to follow to achieve a certain result. If you're baking a cake, you don't just shout "Cake!" and expect one to materialize, no matter how specific you get with your declaration ("with strawberry icing and a caramel filling!"). This would be the declarative approach, and in practice, it sounds more than a little eccentric. To bake a cake, you follow a series of well-defined steps or instructions and have your ingredients and your oven at the ready. This is akin to the imperative approach in programming; it's more hands-on, and sometimes things get messy. But ultimately it gives you more creative control.

## Generating SVG

So if native SVG doesn't allow for the use of algorithms, how do we write SVG using an imperative approach? The answer is we *script* our SVG, and this is where JavaScript and SvJs come into play.

We could script SVG directly in JavaScript without a library, but that too has its challenges, the main one being the verbose boilerplate code we'd have to write. The SvJs library saves us that trouble, making SVG more intuitive and fun to write. Here's an example of a simple SVG (Figure 1-2) written using vanilla JavaScript:

```
const svg = document.createElementNS('<http://www.w3.org/2000/
svg>', 'svg');
svg.setAttribute('width', '150px');
svg.setAttribute('height', '150px');
const div = document.getElementById('container'); div.
appendChild(svg);
const rect = document.createElementNS('<http://www.w3.org/2000/
svg>', 'rect');
rect.setAttribute('x', '0');
rect.setAttribute('y', '0');
rect.setAttribute('width', '150');
rect.setAttribute('height', '150');
rect.setAttribute('fill', 'cornflowerblue');
svg.appendChild(rect);
```

And the following snippet is the equivalent SVG written using
SvJs (don't worry about the details just yet; all you need to note is how
concise it is vs. vanilla JavaScript). The output of this code you can see in
Figure 1-2.

```
const div = document.getElementById('stage');
const svg = new SvJs().set({ width: '150px', height: '150px'
}).addTo(div);
svg.create('rect').set({
  x: 0, y: 0, width: 150, height: 150, fill: 'cornflowerblue'
});
```

***Figure 1-2.*** *A cornflower blue-colored rectangle, in all its glory*

Now you *could* write some functions to make writing vanilla JavaScript less painful, but that leads you down the road of writing a whole host of other utility functions to make the basics less burdensome. With SvJs, I've done my best to save you this trouble. It's essentially a very thin wrapper over the real SVG spec with some helpful generative functions thrown in. This keeps its footprint extremely light while maintaining fidelity to the SVG spec.

SvJs was inspired by the gySVG library, a similarly light but more general-purpose JavaScript library that comes complete with a plug-in API and modern framework support. I was initially going to use gySVG and extend its functionality with a plug-in, but this plug-in soon grew to the point where it made more sense to write my own library with a specific focus on generative art. This was how SvJs came to be.

# Getting Set Up

Enough with the preamble. Let's get ourselves set up to write some code.

## The Code Editor

If you don't have VS Code already running on your machine, head on over to code.visualstudio.com and download and install the appropriate version for your operating system.

If you can't install a code editor on your machine or would just prefer to follow along online, you can use CodePen instead. Go to codepen.io and sign up an account if you're not already registered.

I will be writing the examples throughout this book with the VS Code editor and local files in mind; the same code can be found online via the CodePen versions with some minimal differences (such as how we import the SvJs library and the lack of HTML boilerplate which CodePen automatically provides).

## Node.js and NPM

You can skip this part if you intend to use CodePen only, but I would still recommend getting familiar with Node.js if you have any plans on getting into the field of web development.

Node.js is an open source JavaScript runtime environment that allows you to set up your own JavaScript-powered server. It also allows you to manage dependencies via the included package manager NPM.

Go to nodejs.org and download and install the latest LTS (long-term support) version.

# Initializing and Installing SvJs

Create a base folder where you'll save all the work related to this book, and name it something like `generative-svg`.

Open up VS Code, select File ➤ Open File, and navigate to this folder. Next, select the Terminal ➤ New Terminal command, and you should see a new window appear at the bottom of the screen referencing the current folder location. It should look something like this:

```
your-name@computer-name ~/Documents/generative-svg
```

The important thing is that the path references the folder you created in the last step (i.e., `generative-svg`). Once you've verified that, you're ready to initialize the project. To do this, type the following into the terminal:

```
npm init -y
```

What this does is run Node's package manager NPM, and the `init` command initializes the project, or "package." The `-y` flag just tells `npm` that we want to accept all default setup options. You should notice a new file has been created, called `package.json`. This is a file you'll see a lot of in web development, but you don't need to worry about its contents right now. Just know that its purpose is to manage our dependencies, the main one being the SvJs library.

To install SvJs, run the following command:

```
npm install svjs
```

This will add a new line in the `package.json` file, referencing the version of SvJs you've just installed. A `package-lock.json` file will also be created (a file you'll never need to look at) and a `node_modules` folder, where SvJs and any of its dependencies are stored (it doesn't have any so you won't see additional folders here).

# Scaffolding Our Sketches

Our first sketch will require a little HTML and CSS before we tackle the JavaScript. We'll keep this markup and styling minimal and more or less identical throughout the book, as our real focus will be on the JavaScript.

Let's create a new folder called `sketches` inside the base folder, and inside `sketches` create a new folder called `00-template`. We'll number our folders so that they sort nicely. The `00-template` folder will contain the very basics we'll copy from one sketch to another. Inside `00- template` create a file called `index.html` and another called `sketch.js`. Once you've done that, you should have a folder structure like this:

```
generative-svg
  |-- node_modules
  |-- sketches
    |-- 00-template
       |-- index.html
       |-- sketch.js
  |-- package-lock.json
  |-- package.json
```

Open the `index.html` file. It's worth noting that VS Code can generate some boilerplate markup for you if you type `!` and press the `tab` key, but I'll include our boilerplate in full here so you can copy and paste it. Generally, I recommend you write out the example code yourself and limit the "control-c-control-v" activity where possible, as you're less likely to learn this way. Here, however, it's fine, as HTML and CSS aren't our focus.

```
<!DOCTYPE html>
<html lang="en">
<head>
  <meta charset="UTF-8">
  <meta http-equiv="X-UA-Compatible" content="IE=edge">
```

```
<meta name="viewport" content="width=device-width, initial-
scale=1.0">
<style>
  body {
    margin: 0;
    background-color: #202020;
  }
  #container {
    display: flex;
    justify-content: center;
    align-items: center;
    height: 100vh;
  }
</style>
<title>SvJs Template</title>
</head>
<body>
  <div id="container"></div>
  <script src="./sketch.js" type="module"></script>
</body>
</html>
```

There's just a couple of things worth pointing out about the preceding code: our `<div id="container">` will be where the generative art actually happens. It will be our canvas, so to speak. I have placed it within the center of the screen, removed any default margins, and given the template an overall "dark-mode" feel (my own personal preference).

Below the `<div>` you'll see a `<script>` tag. This is where we'll pull in all our code, so any further modifications to the HTML will be unnecessary going forward (other than maybe updating the `<title>` tag for each sketch, but I'll leave that up to you). The script is set to `type="module"`. What this

11

does is allow us to handle the import of other files and libraries that are packaged (or exported) as modules. This is a good practice to get into, and it's also how we're going to import the SvJs library.

Open up the sketch.js file and include this as your first two lines:

```
// Import the SvJs library.
import { SvJs } from '../../node_modules/svjs/src/index.js';
```

Our template is now complete, ready to be copied for subsequent sketches. Well done!

## Serving Our Sketches

If you navigate to the 00-template folder at this point and double-click on index.html to open it in a web browser, you'll see some errors in the developer console (accessible by pressing F12 on most browsers). This is because we need to serve our HTML files using the http:// protocol rather than the file:// protocol (you'll see the protocol prefix if you check the full URL in the address bar).

To rectify this, we need to install an http server. And ideally one that detects file changes and instantly reloads our page, saving us from having to manually refresh our browser each time (which becomes a pain after a while). There's a neat little package called live-server that takes care of this for us. To install it, run the following in the terminal:

```
npm install live-server -g
```

The -g flag tells npm to install this package globally on our machine, rather than locally to the project in question. As it's more a general-purpose utility than a project-specific dependency, this is what we want.

To get live-server to run, all you need to do is type live-server into the terminal. It will then automatically open a new browser window where you'll see your project files (assuming you're still in the project's base folder in VS Code). Navigate to sketches ➤ 00-template and you should see your page load free of any console errors. It's also free of any content though, so let's write some code to address this.

# Our First Generative Sketch

As I mentioned previously, our first sketch will serve as a basis for explaining the fundamental programming concepts we'll be covering in Chapter 2, so what follows is, for this reason, rather light on explanations (other than some comments in the code itself).

Make a copy of the 00-template folder and call it 01-our-first-generative-sketch, ensuring to copy it to the same location (i.e., so that the parent folder is sketches).

Then, either write out the following code (recommended) or copy it into your sketch.js file, below the import statement. Read the comments as you go (the lines starting with //), which I've purposely kept quite verbose so you can get a better handle on what's happening.

```
// Import the SvJs library.
import { SvJs } from '../../node_modules/svjs/src/index.js';

// Create some global variables.
const svgSize = window.innerWidth > window.innerHeight ?
window.innerHeight : window.innerWidth;
const bgColor = '#181818';

// Create an object to store some of our randomised parameters.
const randomised = {
  hue: random(0, 360),
  rotation: random(-180, 180),
  iterations: random(10, 100)
}
```

```
// Create our parent SVG and attach it to the element with id
'container'.
const svg = new SvJs(); svg.addTo(document.
getElementById('container'));
```

```
// Set the width and height of the viewBox and the displayed
size of the SVG.
svg.set({ viewBox: '0 0 1000 1000', width: svgSize, height:
svgSize });
```

```
// Create a background layer - a rectangle the full size of our
viewBox.
const rect = svg.create('rect');
rect.set({ x: 0, y: 0, width: 1000, height: 1000, fill:
bgColor });
```

```
// Run a loop a random number of times to create our ellipses.
for (let i = 0; i < randomised.iterations; i += 1) {

  // Set the centre point, the x and y radii of our ellipse and
  its rotation.
  let center = 500;
  let radiusX = 100 + (i * 3);
  let radiusY = 300 + (i * 2);
  let rotation = randomised.rotation + (i * 2);
  // If our random hue is less than 180, increment it.
  Otherwise decrement it.
  let hue;
  if (randomised.hue < 180) {
    hue = randomised.hue + (i * 3);
  } else {
    hue = randomised.hue - (i * 3);
  }
```

```
// Create our ellipse.
let ellipse = svg.create('ellipse');
ellipse.set({
    cx: center,
    cy: center,
    rx: radiusX,
    ry: radiusY,
    fill: 'none',
    stroke: `hsl(${hue} 80% 80% / 0.6)`,
    transform: `rotate(${rotation} ${center} ${center})`
  });
}

/**
 * Gets a random number between a minimum and maximum value.
 */
function random(min, max, integer = true) {
  let random = Math.random() * (max - min) + min;
  let number = integer ? Math.floor(random) : random;
  return number;
}
```

Ok, so quite the code dump! It will no doubt overwhelm anyone new to coding, so if you fall into this category and find yourself balking at the aforementioned, please bear with me; all will be explained in the forthcoming chapters. The purpose of this first generative sketch is to just jump in and show you some quick results.

When you save the aforementioned, you should see something like Figure 1-3. Each refresh of the browser will render a unique version, so what you see will no doubt differ in some respects. But that, dear reader, is part of the joy of generative art.

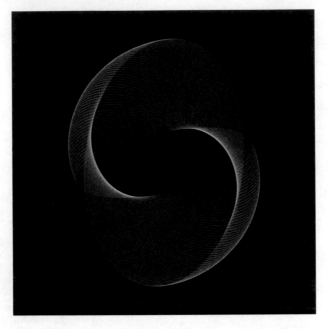

***Figure 1-3.*** *Our first generative sketch (one variation of many)*

## Summary

To recap, we've covered the following in this first chapter:

- Why we're using JavaScript and SvJs rather than Processing or p5.js

- What sets SVG apart from raster formats like PNG and JPG

- How scripting SVG differs from writing it directly in markup

- How SvJs can make SVG scripting more intuitive and less verbose

- Installing and importing the SvJs library and setting up our base template

- How to serve our sketches from a local development server

Coming up next: a programming primer.

# CHAPTER 2

# A Programming Primer

Although programming can be used to create art, it can also be an art in itself. It is part art and part science. When beginning programming, you need to familiarize yourself more with the scientific side of it, the fundamental concepts and rules that comprise programming as a discipline. The art can come later.

Learning the basics in programming means getting to grips with concepts like values, variables, operators, expressions, conditionals, loops, functions, and more. If you have no idea what any of these are, don't worry. That's what this chapter is for.

We'll also cover the characteristics (including some of the peculiarities) of JavaScript, our language of choice. JavaScript is a powerful and enormously popular language; it is the only programming language web browsers natively understand, so naturally enough, it is *everywhere*. Learning JavaScript is therefore a very practical choice and will serve you well in a lot of other areas besides generative art.

## Syntax

We'll begin with some points on syntax.

© David Matthew 2024
D. Matthew, *Generative Art with JavaScript and SVG*, Design Thinking,
https://doi.org/10.1007/979-8-8688-0086-3_2

# Case Sensitivity

JavaScript is a case-sensitive language, so the words `JavaScript` and `javascript` would be considered distinct from one another. A capitalization convention that many coders adhere to when naming functions or variables is something called camel case, where terms are joined together in a manner resembling the humps of a camel. For example:

```
thisIsCamelCase
soIsThis
```

As you can see, the first part of the term is entirely lowercase, and all subsequent terms use what we'd call title case, where the first character of the word is capitalized.

# Spacing

Unlike some languages that enforce strict indentation, whitespace in JavaScript doesn't carry any intrinsic meaning. Spacing is mostly a matter of style. The most prevalent stylistic convention you'll come across within the JavaScript community is the use of two spaces to indent code, as follows:

```
someCode() {
  some indented code
}
```

# Semicolons

Each statement in JavaScript should end with a semicolon ( ; ), which is the equivalent of a full stop in natural language. You can choose to leave them out altogether, due to a JavaScript feature called Automatic

Semicolon Insertion (ASI), but because this isn't always safe to do (and because I also work with other languages where semicolons are mandatory), I opt to leave them in.

The code throughout this book will therefore use semicolons.

# Comments

A very important habit to cultivate is the liberal use of comments in any code you write. Not only so that others can more easily read and understand your code, but so that *you* can do so too. You'd be amazed at how quickly your own code can become conundrum-like without comments to guide the way.

There are two types of comments in JavaScript: single-line comments and multi-line comments. Single-line comments begin with two forward-slashes //, and multi-line comments begin with a forward slash and asterisk /* and terminate with an asterisk and forward slash */.

```
// A single-line comment. Useful for quick explanations.

/*
 * A multi-line comment.
 * Useful for properly documenting code.
 */
```

Single-line comments can also be placed after code on the same line.

```
someCode(); // We can safely write a comment here.
```

# Values

As a programmer, you've got to be well versed in values and their various types. We're not talking moral values here or a programming code of ethics; by values, we mean "chunks" of information that are eventually boiled down to the bytes and bits that the computer processes.

Values can be anything from numbers to strings of text (like "I love breakfast cereals"). Let's start with numbers.

# Numbers

If computers love anything at all, it's numbers. They can crunch them far faster than I can crunch through my favorite breakfast cereal. In some programming languages, there are different types of numbers (e.g., int representing integers or whole numbers and float representing decimal or floating-point numbers), but in JavaScript, all numeric values are of the single type Number.

```
17 // A whole number.
23.085 // A decimal number.
4e2 // A number with an exponent (four to the power of two in
this case).
```

# Strings

Strings represent textual information, like words and sentences. Strings need to be surrounded by quote marks, of the single or double variety.

```
'There are 10 kinds of people in this world.' // Single quotes
"Those who understand binary and those who don't." //
Double quotes
```

Whether you choose to use single or double quotes, it's important to be consistent with your choice. Try not to mix them haphazardly.

Another type of string exists called the template literal, which allows you to insert variables and expressions into a string. This isn't possible with standard single or double quotes. Template literals are surrounded by backticks, and code can be inserted between curly braces prepended by a dollar sign, like so:

```
`Some text here ${someCodeHere}, and more text here. Pretty
cool huh?`
```

This is a more recent feature of JavaScript and is extremely useful for handling concatenated (i.e., pieced together) and multi-line strings. Let's illustrate this with an example.

```
// Here's how developers used to have to store multi-line HTML
string data.
let oldWay = '' +
'    <div class="intro">\n' +
'\n' +
'        <p>My name is ' + name + ' and I am ' + age + ' years
         of age.</p>\n'
'\n' +
'    </div>\n';

// And here's how the same thing can be done now.
let newWay = `
<div class="intro">

    <p>My name is ${name} and I am ${age} years of age.</p>

</div>`;
```

As you can see, it is much more readable and concise. As a rule, whenever you want to mix string values with anything else, backticks are the best choice.

# Booleans

Boolean values are binary; they can be either true or false. They are named after George Boole, inventor of Boolean algebra.

They can be useful for representing any binary state: yes or no, on or off, alive or dead, etc. They are written as simply true or false.

```
let alive = true; // phew
let kicking = false; // just sitting
```

Booleans make conditional statements and comparisons possible, which we'll get to a little later.

# Empty Values

Empty values are the final values we'll consider. There are two: null and undefined. You can think of them as values that carry no information. You'll see a lot of them (particularly undefined) when debugging your code, so as you can imagine, they are not always the most welcome of visitors.

What is the difference between null and undefined? A simplified way to think of it is this: when JavaScript tells you a variable called x is null, it's saying "yeah I know about x, but x doesn't have any value so far as I can see." If, on the other hand, it tells you that x is undefined, it is essentially saying "What the **** is x? Ain't no x around here."

# Variables

We've name-dropped variables a couple of times already, so what exactly are they? You can think of variables like containers for values that can be referenced later.

A variable needs to be declared before it can be used. There are three ways to do this: using `const`, `let`, or `var`.

The latter, `var`, is no longer recommended; I mention it mainly for historical reasons and because it is something you'll likely encounter in the wild. Many, many JavaScript code bases out there still use `var`, simply because prior to the great JavaScript update of 2015 (called ECMAScript 6, or ES6 for short), there was no other options available.

Declaring a variable involves using the keyword, creating a name/identifier, and then assigning it a value using the equals operator.

```
const name = 'David Matthew';
const countryOfBirth = 'Ireland';
let age = 21; // I wish!
```

What's the difference between `const` and `let`? When using `const`, you're declaring a value that shouldn't change. My `countryOfBirth` is an example: this is a historical fact that remains constant. If I later tried to reassign a new value to `countryOfBirth`, this would result in an error:

```
countryOfBirth = 'Brazil'; // uh oh...
-> TypeError: Assignment to constant variable
```

My age, however, is (alas) subject to change, so it can be updated without any issues. Another difference between `const` and `let` is that the latter can be declared without a value, whereas with `const`, a value must be assigned to it when it is first created.

```
let a; // A-ok.
const b; // asking for trouble.
-> Uncaught SyntaxError: Missing initializer in const
declaration
```

When unsure, should you use const or let? The general consensus in the JavaScript community is that you should use const by default and only use let when you think the variable may be assigned a new value later. The reasoning is that this can reduce any unintended value re-assignments, ruling out a potential source of bugs.

# Operators

An operator is a symbol that performs operations on values. We've actually come across one already: the assignment operator ( = ), which assigns a value to a variable. Let's see what other kinds of operators are available to us.

## Arithmetic Operators

As you might have guessed, arithmetic operators allow us to perform mathematical operations. The addition operator ( + ) allows us to add numbers, but it also allows us to concatenate strings.

```
// Adding numbers.
2 + 2
-> 4

// Concatenating strings.
'I am' + ' so smrt'
-> 'I am so smrt'
```

There are also operators for subtraction ( - ), multiplication ( * ), and division ( / ).

```
// Subtracting numbers.
9 - 4
-> 5

// Dividing numbers.
9 / 4
-> 2.25

// Multiplying numbers.
9 * 4
-> 36
```

ES6 introduced an exponentiation operator ( ** ), which allows you to multiply one number by a factor of another (i.e., one number to the power of another).

```
// The exponentiation operator.
2 ** 2
-> 4

2 ** 6
-> 64

2 ** 10
-> 1024
```

And finally, there is the modulo operator ( % ). This divides one number by another and gives you the remainder. This can be especially useful when cycling through arrays (which we'll get to later), or quickly finding out if an unknown quantity is even or odd.

```
// The modulo operator in action.
3 % 3
-> 0

3 % 2
-> 1

12 % 5
-> 2
```

At this point, it's worth mentioning rules of precedence, which determine the order in which operations are carried out. The mnemonic BEMDAS can help us out here.

- **B**rackets: Whatever is in brackets or parentheses is evaluated first.

- **E**xponents: Evaluate any exponents next.

- **M**ultiplication and **D**ivision: Next, multipliers and divisors. These two have equal precedence, so they are evaluated in the order they are written, i.e., left to right.

- **A**ddition and **S**ubtraction: Add and subtract any remaining numbers. As with multiplication and division, these have equal precedence and are evaluated left to right.

```
// These sums look similar but result in different answers.
4 / 2 * 2 + 4
-> 8

4 / 2 * (2 + 4)
-> 12

4 / 2 ** 2 + 4
-> 5
```

When in doubt, use parentheses to group operations. This can also improve readability.

# Comparison Operators

As the name suggests, comparison operators compare values. They always return a boolean, that is, a true or false value.

- < is the "less than" operator.

- <= is the "less than or equal to" operator.

- > is the "more than" operator.

- >= is the "more than or equal to" operator.

- == is the "equal to" operator.

- === is the "strictly equal to" operator.

Because of some subtle quirks with how JavaScript works, I would recommend sticking with the strict versions of the equality operators. This can reduce unexpected surprises (i.e., bugs).

```
// Some examples of comparison operators in action.
1 > 2
-> false

2 < 3
-> true

3 <= 4
-> true

5 == "5"
-> true // but not really.

5 === "5"
-> false // that's more like it.
```

# Logical Operators

Lastly, there are the logical operators *and* ( && ), *or* ( || ), and *not* ( ! ). These emulate the conjunction, disjunction, and negation of classical logic.

When conjoining two conditions with &&, the result is true if and only if both conditions are true.

```
true && false
-> false

false && true
-> false

true && true
-> true
```

When using the disjunction (fancy word for *or*), first make sure you use the right characters on your keyboard. The | character is not a capital *i* or lowercase *L*; it's what's known as the pipe character. Depending on your regional keyboard layout, it might be located near either your Enter key or your Shift key.

When using ||, the result is true if one or both conditions are true. This makes intuitive sense if we remember that we are essentially asking the computer "is at least one of these conditions true?"

```
true || false
-> true

false || true
-> true

false || false
-> false
```

Finally, we have the negation operator !. This "flips" the condition immediately following it. It can also be uniquely coupled with the equality operator to mean not equal to ( !== ).

```
!true
-> false

!false
-> true

1 !== 2
-> true

!(2 > 1)
-> false
```

A common source of error for new programmers is using a single pipe character | or a single ampersand & instead of the two together. By themselves, these characters perform bitwise operations (i.e., they manipulate binary values) and are for advanced programming only.

# Conditional Statements

Now that we have comparative and logical operators under our belt, we can proceed to conditionals. A conditional statement in JavaScript allows us to influence a program's control flow. As an analogy, think of rush hour traffic at a four-way intersection, the pavements packed with pedestrians. Without some way to control the flow of traffic, mayhem would ensue. Here is where conditionals are needed, such as the various rules that might underpin a traffic light system.

```
// The basic syntax.
if (conditionIsTrue) {
  // ... run some code
}
```

31

```
// A simplistic pedestrian crossing conditional.
if (pedestrianBtnIsPressed) {
  wait(30s);
  activateRedLights();
  wait(3s);
  activateGreenManSignal();
}
```

To the basic if statement, we can append else and else if conditions too.

```
if (a > b) {
  doThis();
} else if (a === b) {
  doThat();
} else {
  doOtherThing();
}
```

If a given condition isn't true, the code inside its curly braces doesn't get executed. Let's take the preceding example again, with the values filled in for a and b.

```
let a = 3;
let b = 4;
```

```
if (a > b) {
  doThis(); // condition wasn't true, so this code doesn't run.
} else if (a === b) {
  doThat(); // this code also doesn't run.
} else {
  doOtherThing(); // both the above are false, so this
code runs.
}
```

The last conditional form I want to cover is the ternary operator. As its name suggests, it is technically an operator, but because it plays the role of a conditional check, I felt it was more appropriate to include it here.

```
// The basic structure of the ternary operator.
conditionA ? expressionIfTrue : expressionIfFalse;
```

In the aforementioned, we're asking "Is conditionA true? If so, run expressionIfTrue. Otherwise, run expressionIfFalse."

The ternary operator is best used when you want to assign a value to a variable based on whether a certain condition holds true. If that condition doesn't hold true, we then assign it a different value. This is exactly what I used it for in our first generative sketch:

```
const svgSize = window.innerWidth > window.innerHeight ?
window.innerHeight : window.innerWidth;
```

Here, we're saying "If the window's innerWidth is greater than its innerHeight, assign the innerHeight to svgSize. Otherwise, assign to it the innerWidth."

# Loops

Loops are one of a programmer's superpowers. We're talking sea-parting, earth-splitting powers. Or, at the very least, the ability to send your programs spiralling toward infinity, potentially freezing any open browser windows and spinning your CPU fan into a frenzy.

This is because loops can repeat blocks of code over and over, as many times as we want, or indefinitely if needed. However, it's usually wise to set a limit to looping behavior (infinite loops are more often an error than an aim). We set a limit to a loop with what's called a terminating condition, that is, a condition that tells the loop when to stop.

We'll cover two main kinds of loops here: the `while` loop and the `for` loop.

## The While Loop

The `while` loop is the simpler of the two. It's basic structure is as follows:

```
while (condition === true) {
  // run code here while condition is true.
}
```

Now, if the condition in question *always* evaluates to `true`, that would lead to an infinite loop. An important ingredient therefore in any looping structure is a value that changes while the loop is running. This is normally a number that either increments or decrements and is known as an iterator. By convention, `i` tends to be used as the variable name.

```
// Set up the iterator.
let i = 0;

while (i <= 99) {
  // Write the value of i to the browser console.
  console.log(i);
  // Increment i by 1 each time the loop runs.
  i = i + 1;
}
```

The preceding loop will run 100 times, starting at 0 and continuing until it is less than or equal to 99, and on each iteration, it will log the value of `i` to the browser console. If we left out the code to increment `i`, it would loop indefinitely.

It's worth noting at this point that there are shorthand ways of incrementing and decrementing – or indeed multiplying and dividing – variable values:

```
// Long way.
i = i + 1
i = i * 2
i = i - 1
i = i / 2

// Shorter way.
i += 1
i *= 2
i -= 1
i /= 2

// Even shorter way (only valid for adding or
subtracting by 1).
i++
i--
```

The shorthand notation is what you'll likely encounter in practice, so we'll continue to use it here.

## The For Loop

The for loop uses the same logic as our example while loop but bakes the iterator and incrementation into a single line. Its typical structure is as follows:

```
for (let i = startingNumber; i < upperLimit; i += increment) {
    // run some code while i is less than the upperLimit.
}
```

The for loop structure is succinctly divided into three sections. We first initialize the iterator, then set the terminating condition, and then decide how we're going to vary the iterator. Here's the for loop version of our previous example, where we logged the value of i to the browser console on each iteration.

```
for (let i = 0; i <= 99; i++) {
  console.log(i);
}
```

You don't always have to increment the iterator. You can just as easily reverse the loop and have it count down from 99 to 0 by making a few tweaks.

```
for (let i = 99; i >= 0; i--) {
  console.log(i);
}
```

It is common to use the value of the iterator in the body of the for loop in combination with other variables to achieve some dynamic result. In our opening generative sketch for example, I used i to progressively increase the radiusX and radiusY of each ellipse.

```
// Run a loop (a randomised number of times) to create our
ellipses.
for (let i = 0; i < randomised.iterations; i += 1) {
  // ... code.
  let radiusX = 100 + (i * 3);
  let radiusY = 300 + (i * 2);
  // ... more code.
}
```

There's lots more to love about loops, and other variations also exist (such as the for in, the for of, and the forEach which we'll cover later), but for the purposes of generative art, we'll be mainly utilizing the standard for loop.

# Functions

Functions are fundamental to JavaScript as a language and are perhaps the single most important concept we'll cover in this chapter. Functions are self-contained blocks of code that perform a particular task. The task is defined in the function body, and it might range from adding two numbers together to initiating a rocket launch sequence.

Standard functions are defined using the function keyword followed by the name you give it, which is then appended with parentheses and opening and closing curly braces where the task is defined.

```
// Basic syntax of a standard function.
function peformSomeTask() {
  // ... code defining the task.
}
```

# Function Parameters

Although functions are used in a wide variety of ways, their primary purpose is to make code reusable. One way to do this is to add parameters to the function, which are defined within the parentheses of the function name.

```
// A function with parameters.
function sayHello(name) {
  // Greet the user the Irish way.
  console.log(`Howaya ${name}, what's the craic?`);
}
```

Functions may or may not explicitly return a value, and if they do, only one return value is allowed. In the preceding example, a value isn't returned, as that isn't the purpose of the function (or to get technical about it, an undefined value would be returned if the function was queried). In the following example, however, we are specifically looking to get a value returned from the function, and this is where we use the return keyword.

```
// Another function with parameters, this time returning
a value.
function squareNumber(number) {
  return number * number;
}
```

The preceding function, when called, will return the result we're looking for, that is, the square of the number we supply it. But how do we actually do this in practice?

# Invoking Functions

To use a function we've defined, we need to invoke it. This is synonymous with calling or executing the function. It can be done like so:

```
// Invoking a function.
performSomeTask();
```

To invoke a function that has parameters as part of its definition, we supply it with arguments. Arguments are the actual values we give the function when we invoke it. The parameters, on the other hand, are how we define these values. Let's see how we might invoke a function with arguments.

```
sayHello('Dave');
-> "Howaya Dave, what's the craic?"

console.log(squareNumber(4));
-> 16
```

Here, we've provided the argument 'Dave' for the first function and 4 for the second, and we've received the expected output. But what if we called the function and forgot the arguments? Let's try it out.

```
sayHello();
-> "Howaya undefined, what's the craic?"

squareNumber();
-> NaN
```

We've encountered undefined before, but not NaN. This just means "not a number." In both cases, our functions don't work so well without arguments. How might we fix this and make them a little more resilient?

One straightforward way is to assign default values when defining a function's parameters. Let's rewrite our sayHello() function as an example.

```
function sayHello(name = ", ah it's yourself") {
  // Greet the user the Irish way.
  console.log(`Howaya ${name}, what's the craic?`);
}

sayHello();
-> "Howaya, ah it's yourself, what's the craic?"
```

As you can see, creating a default value is as simple as assigning a value to the parameter when you define it. Now we've created a more human-sounding fallback than undefined.

In the case of the squareNumber() function, a default value doesn't make as much sense. Instead, we could use the ternary technique covered earlier to provide some actionable feedback if the function is called without an argument.

```
function squareNumber(number) {
  return number ? number * number : 'Please include the number
  you want to square';
}
```

In the squareNumber() function body, our ternary operator is essentially asking "Is number defined? If so, return the result of multiplying it by itself; otherwise, return our fallback message."

At this point, you should be in a better position to fully understand the function defined in our first generative sketch. Have another look and see if it makes more sense now.

```
function random(min, max, integer = true) {
  let random = Math.random() * (max - min) + min;
  let number = integer ? Math.floor(random) : random;
  return number;
}
```

## Scope

The scope of a variable refers to its visibility, or where in a program the variable can be accessed. It's particularly important to be aware of when working with functions.

If, for example, we defined a variable within a function, it would only be visible within that function.

```
function scopeTest() {
  const a = 1;
}

console.log(a);
-> Uncaught ReferenceError: a is not defined
```

However, if we defined the same variable outside that function, it would be visible from *within* the function.

```
const a = 1;

function scopeTest() {
  console.log(a);
}

scopeTest();
-> 1
```

In the first case, the variable is block-scoped, that is, confined to the block of the function. In the latter case, the variable is defined globally (outside all functions) and can be accessed anywhere in the program.

Although it may seem more beneficial to be able to access a variable from anywhere within a program, we should exercise caution where global variables are concerned. In general, it is better to explicitly restrict the scope of our variables. This is one of the main reasons why var has been deprecated, as it can't be "contained" in the same way that let and const can be.

```
function scopeTest() {
  var a = 1;
}

console.log(a);
-> 1
```

As you can see earlier, when using var, the variable can break out of the surrounding block, and this can be problematic in larger programs.

When coding generative art, we're usually writing relatively small programs (or "sketches") and global variables aren't as much of an issue. However, we'll discuss in the next section how best to make certain settings globally available throughout our sketches without relying on global variables.

## Anonymous Functions

Functions don't always have to have a name. Particularly when working with events and callbacks (which we'll cover in a later chapter), functions are often called anonymously as function expressions, executed in order to return a value. Anonymous functions can also be assigned to variables that then store the returned value.

```
// An anonymous function expression assigned to a variable.
const sum = function(a, b) {
  return a + b;
}
```

In the preceding example, the variable can be used to execute the function.

```
sum(5, 4);
-> 9
```

One thing we cannot do with anonymous functions is use them at the start of a statement.

```
// The below is a no-no.
function(a, b) {
  return a + b;
}
-> Uncaught SyntaxError: Function statements require a
function name
```

## Arrow Functions

So far we've covered functions declared with the function keyword, but there is another, more modern way of writing functions. These functions are called arrow functions due to the arrow syntax they employ.

```
// Basic syntax of an arrow function.
const peformSomeTask = () => {
  // ... code defining the task.
}
```

They are concise alternatives to the traditional function expressions we've just covered. Let's rewrite the sum() function as an example.

```
const sum = (a, b) => {
  return a + b;
}
```

A little shorter, as you can see. But it can get even more concise than this if our function only consists of a single statement that returns a value (which exactly describes our sum() function). In such a case, we don't need the curly braces or even the return statement itself.

```
const sum = (a, b) => a + b;
```

Because the arrow function body consists of just a single statement ( a + b ), it is assumed we want the value of this statement returned. This is what's called an implicit return.

Now, not all arrow functions can be so neatly condensed, just those that have a single return statement. But such one-liners are liberally used throughout most modern JavaScript code bases, particularly those that use declarative front-end frameworks like React, so it's worth familiarizing yourself with them.

There is another reason to use arrow functions that stretches a little beyond the scope of this chapter, and it's this. What I mean is the this keyword, which is a complicated topic in JavaScript (and complicated to explain without getting tangled in reflexive language). Suffice to say, the value of this is more predictable and less prone to bugs when used in arrow functions. But don't worry about this for now.

Instead, let's concern ourselves with some data structures that will serve us well in generative art and in JavaScript more generally. This is the subject of our next section.

# Objects and Arrays

Variables are great when you need to define values like numbers, strings, and booleans, but what if you need a more sophisticated way to represent and organize your data? Say you have a long list of things – be they this week's groceries, the employees in your company, the locations you want to visit before you kick the proverbial bucket, or, to bring it back to generative art, the hexadecimal codes of the 216 web-safe colors you'd like to sample for your next retro-inspired masterpiece (in the 1990s, web developers – or web masters as they were then known – had a much more restricted color palette).

When you have lists of anything, arrays are your friend.

# Arrays

An array is essentially a variable that can contain multiple values. And in JavaScript, these values needn't be of a uniform type. This means we can mix numbers, strings, and booleans into a single array if required (though it's not necessarily recommended you do this).

Arrays take the following format:

```
// The syntax of a standard array.
let arrayName = [item1, item2, item3, ... itemN];
```

Each array item has a corresponding index, or number, that represents its position in the array. The first item in an array has an index of 0 (counting from zero in computing is the norm), the second item has an index of 1, the third of 2, etc. To directly access an item in array by its index, you use square bracket notation like so:

```
// Access the first item.
let firstItem = arrayName[0];

// Access the second item.
let secondItem = arrayName[1];

// Access the nth item.
let nthItem = arrayName[n + 1];
```

This lends itself particularly well to loops. Iterating over items in an array with a for loop is a very common practice, and it's something we'll lean on heavily throughout our generative art journey.

Let's continue with our web-safe colors example and iterate over an array containing these 216 hexadecimal values.

You don't need to worry about how we get these items into the array for now; all we're interested in is how we'd loop through them and take some action for each item in the array. The action in this case will be to set the color (i.e., fill ) of a newly created circle on each iteration. And to make sure we do this 216 times, we use the length property of the array to control how many times we run our loop.

```
for (let i = 0; i < webSafeColours.length; i += 1) {
  // ... some code.
  circle.fill(webSafeColours[i]);
  // ... more code.
}
```

In Figure 2-1, you'll see the output of this code snippet. Obviously there's more involved in achieving this spiral arrangement (something we'll cover in a later chapter); the main point is how we use the iterator variable i to cycle through each color value, that is, webSafeColours[i].

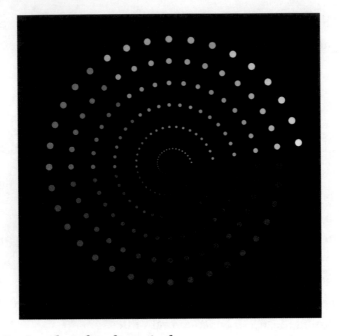

***Figure 2-1.*** *A web-safe color spiral*

If you're brave enough to inspect the code behind the example, you'll notice that to add each color to the array initially, I used an array method called push(). The relevant line is

```
colours.push(colour);
```

The push() method is how we add an item to the end of an array (think of loading a truck from the back). If instead we wanted to add the item to the beginning of the array, we'd use a method called unshift().

```
colours.unshift(colour);
```

If we wanted to remove an item from the end of the array, we'd use the pop() method (think popcorn popping out of a pot). Conversely, if we wanted to remove an item from the beginning of the array, we'd use the shift() method (so-called because we're shifting all remaining items to a lower index).

There's one other method I want to cover before moving on, namely, the forEach() loop I mentioned earlier. This method is unique to arrays and acts on each item of the array in turn, using a function as its argument. As an aside, functions that are passed as arguments in this manner are known as callback functions.

```
// Set up an sample array.
const someNumbers = [2, 4, 6, 8, 10];
```

```
// Call the forEach method on each array item.
someNumbers.forEach((item) => {
  console.log(item * 2);
});
```

```
-> 4 8 12 16 20
```

The forEach() loop can be a nice succinct way of iterating over an array if the main purpose of the loop is to perform some action specifically for each array item.

## Objects

Objects are another data structure JavaScript offers, and like functions, they are a foundational feature of the language. Take a peek under the hood and you'll find objects everywhere. Functions are, in fact, special kinds of objects.

Like arrays, objects can contain multiple values. The primary difference is that objects label their values with names, whereas arrays label their values with numbers (i.e., the index of each item).

An object takes the following format:

```
const objectName = {
  name1: value1,
  name2: value2,
  name3: value3
};
```

These name-value pairs are the object's **properties**. The values can be anything you want: strings, booleans, functions, arrays, or even other objects. Almost anything you can think of can be represented as an object. Let's take my laptop as an example.

```
const myLaptop = {
  processor: "Core i5",
  screenSize: "14 inches",
  inSleepMode: false,
  powerUp: function() {
    if (inSleepMode) {
      wakeUp();
    } else {
      runBIOS();
    }
  }
  // etc
}
```

With these properties in place, we can call them with either bracket notation, or – more commonly – dot notation.

```
// Accessing an object property with dot notation.
myComputer.screenSize;
-> "14 inches"
```

```
// Accessing via bracket notation.
myComputer[processor];
-> "Core i5"
```

We can also update and create new object properties via the same syntax.

```
// Updating an object's property.
myComputer.inSleepMode = true;
```

```
// Creating a new object property.
myComputer.storage = "512 GB SSD";
```

If you take a look back at our first sketch again, you'll notice that I used an object to store some randomized settings that are later called in the sketch:

```
...
const randomised = {
  hue: random(0, 360),
  rotation: random(-180, 180),
  iterations: random(10, 100)
}
...
let rotation = randomised.rotation + (i * 2);
```

This is a good way of getting around the issue of global variables I mentioned earlier. Using an object, we can make our settings globally available without relying on global variables. This can keep our code tidier and less likely to cause conflicts.

# Classes

A class is like a blueprint, or template, for creating objects. The objects that are created are then said to be *instances* of that class. A class can include both data and functions to work on that data. This coupling of data and code is referred to as encapsulation.

We won't be going into much detail with classes, but it will be useful to know some basic terminology, as the SvJs library we'll be using is class based.

To create an instance of a class, we use the new keyword, followed by the class name with brackets. This calls the class constructor.

```
// Defining a class.
class StarShip {
   ...
}

// Instantiating (or constructing) a class.
const prometheus = new StarShip();
```

Functions that are part of a class are known as methods. A class will usually have, at the very least, methods to get and set its properties.

```
prometheus.setDestination = 'Moon LV-223, Zeta 2 Reticuli';
prometheus.takeOff();
```

When we created our first generative SVG in Chapter 1, we began by creating an SvJs class instance and calling some of its methods.

```
const svg = new SvJs();
svg.addTo(document.getElementById('container'));
```

This is the extent to which we will be working with classes; writing them won't be part of this book.

# Idiosyncrasies and Other Features

JavaScript offers plenty of other features, including closures, error catching, proxies, promises, and more, but I can't cover them all here. What I will point out here are some of the oddities – or quirks if we're being kinder – associated with JavaScript that may confound coders coming from another language.

# Null and NaN Weirdness

We learned previously that null is essentially the absence of information. Isn't it strange then that null is also considered an object? We can confirm this by using the typeof check.

```
typeof null;
-> object
```

Despite this, null is not considered an instance *of* an object. We can confirm this by using the instanceof check.

```
null instanceof Object;
-> false
```

NaN (not a number) also presents us with some quantum-level weirdness that would have Schrodinger's cat perk up its ears. It is apparently not a number but equal to a number at the same time. And, bizarrely, not even equal to itself.

```
typeof NaN;
-> Number
```

```
NaN === Number;
-> false
```

```
NaN === NaN
-> false
```

# Secret Casting

JavaScript does some things behind the scenes that programmers from stricter languages may not always appreciate. It is, for example, notoriously loose with data types and will convert variables of different types into matching types to suit the situation (the process of converting a data type is also known as casting it). Let's play with some numbers as an example.

```
1 == 1;
-> true

1 == "1";
-> true
```

How can a number equal a string? Well, it can't. JavaScript is casting the string as a number to make sense of the expression. It is essentially coercing the string data into number data (also known as type coercion). That's why we're always better off using the strict equality operator in JavaScript, something that doesn't exist in many other languages.

```
1 === "1";
-> false
```

This kind of casting also occurs when we try to add numbers to strings, but it works in the opposite direction; the numbers in this case are converted to strings.

```
1 + "2";
-> "12"

"2" + 3;
-> "23"
```

To avoid the pitfalls of this kind of implicit type coercion, functions like parseInt(), parseFloat(), and toString() can be used to re-cast or explicitly convert variables to the data type you want to work with.

## Semicolon Uncertainty

I mentioned at the start of the chapter that you can write JavaScript without semicolons if you wish, but that in some edge cases, it can result in unexpected behavior. Here's one such edge case.

```
return
1 + 2
-> undefined
```

Spacing doesn't matter in JavaScript, so what is going on here? Why isn't the expression returning 3? Well, here the Automatic Semicolon Insertion feature is being invoked under the hood. The actual code being evaluated is this:

```
return;
1 + 2;
```

To avoid this, either familiarize yourself with such edge cases or just use semicolons.

## Summary

We've covered a lot in this chapter:

- Basic rules of JavaScript syntax

- Values, such as strings, numbers, and booleans

- Variables and the different ways to declare them

- Arithmetic, comparison, and logical operators

- Conditional statements and control flow

- While loops, for loops, and forEach loops

- Functions and scope

- Arrays and array methods

- Objects and object properties, and alternatives to global variables

- Some of JavaScript's quirkier features

I've assumed next to no coding knowledge, so if that describes your starting point and you've still kept up, well done!

In the next chapter, we'll explore the main functionality of the SvJs library and get comfortable creating basic shapes, lines, and colors.

# CHAPTER 3

# All About SVG

With the basics of JavaScript under your belt, you're now ready for SvJs, which you can think of as your generative brush and palette.

In this chapter, we'll cover setting up our SVG canvas; how to work with line and color; how to create a range of simple shapes; how to add text and titles; how to define and reuse elements; how to use groups, gradients, and patterns; and how the SVG viewBox and viewport work; and in the process, we'll learn the core functions of the SvJs library and how it relates to the SVG spec.

## The Parent SVG Element

Before we can create anything visually, we need to load our library and set up the parent SVG element. The parent SVG, or the SVG document fragment as it's also known, is that SVG element whose parent element (if it has one) is not in the SVG namespace. An example would be an SVG attached to an HTML DOM node.

```
<div id="container">
    <svg></svg>
</div>
```

This is worth mentioning only because SVGs can contain other SVGs; in these cases, only one of those can be considered the parent SVG element. You might also see this referred to as the root element.

© David Matthew 2024
D. Matthew, *Generative Art with JavaScript and SVG*, Design Thinking,
https://doi.org/10.1007/979-8-8688-0086-3_3

Let's reopen the JavaScript template file we set up in Chapter 1 (it should be located in sketches/00-template/sketch.js) and add the following line to it:

```
// Parent SVG.
const svg = new SvJs();
```

The new SvJs() constructor, if called without any arguments, creates an SVG element. It can also be used to create any other SVG element by passing in the name of that element as a string.

```
// Using the SvJs constructor to create a circle element.
const circle = new SvJs('circle');
```

To add our parent SVG element to our web page, we use the SvJs addTo() method. In this case, we'll pass in the <div> with the id of container that we set up earlier in our HTML (see Chapter 1). Add the following to the template sketch:

```
const container = document.getElementById('container'); svg.
addTo(container);
```

Most functions in SvJs are chainable, meaning you can chain them together using dot notation, like so:

```
methodOne().methodTwo();
```

The new SvJs() constructor method is no exception, so our new parent SVG element can actually be immediately attached to a DOM element once instantiated, by appending the addTo() method to it. This creates a method chain (think of the dot as the link). And if we pass the getElementById() DOM method as an argument instead of assigning it to a variable, we can condense our code down to a single line:

```
// Parent SVG.
const svg = new SvJs().addTo(document.
getElementById('container'));
```

56

Concision doesn't always beat clarity however, so if this one-liner is a little too compressed for your liking, keep your template code as is, no need to replace it with the aforementioned.

# The Viewport and ViewBox

The viewport refers to the visible portion of our SVG element. It is defined implicitly, via the use of width and height attributes.

One of the interesting things about the SVG format is its flexibility with regard to its workspace, that is, the areas in which it can contain content. An SVG may contain much more besides what is visible at any one time through the viewport. This opens up the possibility of working with sprites, artboards, and other offscreen assets.

Because we'll be working with a square SVG viewport, our width and height will be the same, so we can use a single variable to store this value. We'll call this svgSize. We don't know in advance what the screen size or orientation will be, so hard-coding a value wouldn't be wise. Instead, we can check the browser window dimensions by querying window.innerWidth and window.innerHeight and set svgSize to the smaller of the two values. This will ensure a square (or 1:1) aspect ratio. The ternary operator that we covered in the previous chapter is particularly useful for these kinds of checks. Include it as follows in the template to initialize the svgSize variable:

```
// Viewport size (1:1 aspect ratio).
const svgSize = window.innerWidth > window.innerHeight ?
window.innerHeight : window.innerWidth;
```

The viewBox is another important top-level SVG attribute. It is related to the viewport but has more powerful (and more complex) capabilities. The viewBox allows us to define the position and dimensions of our viewport in user space.

What does this mean exactly? Well, you can think of user space as unitless, or unit-independent, space. A value of 100 might refer to pixels, millimeters, meters, or any other unit. It will default to pixels, but the point of the viewBox is that it can free us from thinking in absolute units. We can work with our own internal coordinate system without worrying about the actual dimensions of the device used to render the SVG.

Personally, I like working with a width and height of 1000, as I find it intuitive to divide up a canvas that way. Those 1000 units could later be squeezed into a square 500px wide, or splashed across a billboard the size of a bus.

The first two values of the viewBox define its starting coordinates (known as min-x and min-y), and the second two define the width and height. We'll keep things simple by defining the viewBox as 0 0 1000 1000.

If the viewport and viewBox don't share the same aspect (i.e., width to height) ratio, the preserveAspectRatio attribute can be used to specify how the browser should display the SVG. This can get complex quite quickly, which is why I've already ensured our viewport and viewBox will share the same 1:1 (i.e., square) aspect ratio. For now, just be aware the preserveAspectRatio attribute exists, should you wish to facilitate more elaborate setups in future.

Sometimes to best understand how something works, you need to visually interact with it. With that in mind, I built a little CodePen sketch (or "pen" as they're called) demonstrating the effect of adjusting the main viewBox values, so you can see how they can be used together to scale and crop the content visible within the SVG viewport. You can find the pen at davidmatthew.ie/generative-art-javascript-svg#viewBox

At this point, we have the values we need for our viewBox and viewport, but we haven't yet learned how to put them to use.

# Setting and Getting Values

Every SvJs instance, whether it's the parent SVG or one of its child elements, has a set() method. This method allows us to set the values of an element's attributes.

How do we know what attributes an element has? Well, we'd consult (i.e., google) some official documentation. The source I'd recommend is the Mozilla Developer Network's SVG element reference, available at developer.mozilla.org/en-US/docs/Web/SVG/Element. Use it for reminders or for when you do your own independent explorations. And while we're at it, the full documentation for the SvJs  library is available at npmjs.com/package/svjs (or at the related GitHub repository); if you'd prefer, have that to hand for a more structured definition of each method.

Getting back to setting values, the set() method accepts an object as its argument and takes the following format:

```
svg.set({ attribute1: value1, attribute2: value2, attributeN:
valueN )};
```

If you're setting a large number of properties at once, you might consider adjusting the formatting for the sake of readability.

```
svg.set({
  attribute1: value1,
  attribute2: value2,
  ...
  attributeN: valueN
)};
```

It's up to you however; either way works.

The attributes of note for our parent SVG are the width and height (which constitute the viewport) and the viewBox. We can now add the following code to our template to set these attributes:

```
svg.set({ width: svgSize, height: svgSize, viewBox: '0 0 1000
1000' });
```

If you run the live-server command and navigate to our template folder, you'll just see a blank page at this point. This is because our SVG canvas doesn't contain anything to distinguish it from the background. We'll address this shortly by creating a rectangle to act as a background layer/canvas.

Just as we can set() values, we can also get() them. It's unlikely you'll find yourself doing this too often, but it's good to be aware the functionality exists. The following code, for example, outputs our viewBox value to the console:

```
console.log(svg.get('viewBox'));
```

Fetching attribute values via the get() method can be useful when working with event listeners, or in other cases where the values are being updated dynamically.

# Quicker Element Creation

If we had to call the new SvJs constructor and the addTo method each time we created a new SVG element, it might get a little tiresome after a while. This is where the SvJs create() method comes in, as it combines these two steps into one. To create an element and automatically append it to our parent SVG, we'd simply write

```
svg.create('elementName');
```

When creating an element, it's usually best to assign it to a variable in the process, unless you're sure you won't need a reference to it again later. You might therefore write the aforementioned as

```
const variableName = svg.create('elementName');
```

The `create()` method is chainable and can be called by child elements too.

# Lines and Shapes

The SVG spec defines six primitive shape types:

- Circles
- Ellipses
- Lines
- Polygons
- Polylines
- Rectangles

As we need to set up a background, let's start with the rectangle.

# Rectangles and Squares

A rectangle is a `rect` in the SVG spec, so to create one, we'd write

```
svg.create('rect');
```

Next, we'll chain the `set()` method, focusing on the following five attributes of the `rect` element: `x` and `y` to set the position of its top left corner; `width` and `height` to define its size; and `fill` to define its color.

As we want a square rectangle (as a square is technically just a special kind of rectangle), we just need to set our width and height to the same value. Add the following code to our template:

```
// Background.
svg.create('rect').set({
  x: 0, y: 0, width: 1000, height: 1000, fill: '#181818'
});
```

Note that we're defining our background's position and dimensions relative to the viewBox, not the viewport. This keeps our values consistent, as we don't know in advance what size our viewport will be. If you run live-server now, you should see a square canvas just a subtle shade darker than the surrounding background.

This will suffice for our template. In case you've missed anything earlier or just want to ensure your code is in order, here's the template sketch.js file in full:

```
import { SvJs } from '../../node_modules/svjs/src/index.js';

// Parent SVG.
const svg = new SvJs().addTo(document.
getElementById('container'));

// Viewport and viewBox (1:1 aspect ratio).
const svgSize = window.innerWidth > window.innerHeight ?
window.innerHeight : window.innerWidth;
svg.set({ width: svgSize, height: svgSize, viewBox: '0 0 1000
1000' });

// Background.
svg.create('rect').set({
  x: 0, y: 0, width: 1000, height: 1000, fill: '#181818'
});
```

Any further code we write will be specific to the sketch we're working on. Make sure you've saved your changes before copying the `00-template` folder and its contents, renaming it to `02-basic-shapes`.

# First Strokes

There are two important attributes that can be used on practically every graphical SVG element (i.e., elements that are intended to appear on screen). These are an element's `fill` and `stroke`. As we've already seen, the `fill` defines an element's interior color (or background). The `stroke`, on the other hand, defines the color of an element's outline (or border).

If you don't define a `stroke`, none will appear. And if you do define one, its `stroke-width` will default to 1. The `stroke-width` attribute is important to highlight for another reason: it's an example of a hyphenated attribute. We can't use hyphens when setting attributes in JavaScript, as they will be interpreted as subtraction operators.

We have two options to deal with this: we can turn them into strings, that is, write `'stroke-width'` instead of `stroke-width`, or we can replace hyphens with underscores, that is, `stroke-width` becomes `stroke_width`. The latter option is facilitated by SvJs, and it's the solution I prefer; it's faster and looks less out of place than having stringified object properties mixed with others that aren't strings.

Enough with the theory for now – let's create something! The following sketch is a Josef Albers–inspired color illusion and shows that with just plain rectangles, it's possible to create a somewhat interesting composition (illustrated in Figure 3-1).

```
import { SvJs } from '../../node_modules/svjs/src/index.js';

// Viewport size (1:1 aspect ratio).
const svgSize = window.innerWidth > window.innerHeight ?
window.innerHeight :
window.innerWidth;
```

```
// Parent SVG.
const svg = new SvJs().addTo(document.
getElementById('container'));
svg.set({ width: svgSize, height: svgSize, viewBox: '0 0 1000
1000' });

// Background.
svg.create('rect').set({
  x: 0, y: 0, width: 1000, height: 1000, fill: '#181818'
});

// Main orange square.
svg.create('rect').set({
  x: 150, y: 200, width: 700, height: 600, rx: 15, fill:
  '#e56411',
  stroke: '#fff', stroke_width: 30, paint_order: 'stroke'
});

// Blue rectangle.
svg.create('rect').set({
  x: 650, y: 200, width: 200, height: 600, rx: 15, fill:
  '#69969f'
});

// Smaller orange rectangle.
svg.create('rect').set({
  x: 200, y: 425, width: 600, height: 150, rx: 20, fill:
  '#b84b08'
});

// Yellow rectangle.
svg.create('rect').set({
  x: 325, y: 200, width: 175, height: 600, fill: '#fed322'
});
```

```
// Purple rectangle.
svg.create('rect').set({
  x: 500, y: 200, width: 175, height: 600, fill: '#49283c'
});
```

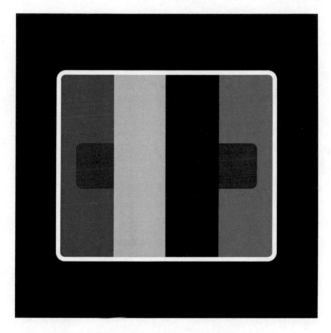

***Figure 3-1.***  *A Josef Albers–inspired color illusion*

Do the smaller rectangles on the right and left look like the same shade of orange? Assuming this illusion was successful, you might have some trouble settling on a definite answer. But by browsing the code, you can easily verify that they are not only the same shade, but the same shape!

What gives the rectangles those rounded corners is the rx attribute, which means its radius on the x axis. If the corresponding ry attribute isn't defined, it's assumed you want the same value (resulting in a uniformly curved corner).

You also might have spotted another hyphenated attribute in the preceding code, namely, `paint-order`. This determines in what order our `fill` and `stroke` are rendered for a given element.

The default order has `fill` come first (i.e., the fill is beneath so it will get partly painted over by the `stroke`), but sometimes it can be useful to have `stroke` come first, as only then will we see the full `fill` dimensions painted (remove `paint_order: 'stroke'` from the code and you'll see what I mean).

## Circles and Ellipses

The circle is the simplest (and arguably the most perfect) of all shapes. We define the position of its center via `cx` and `cy` attributes and its radius via the `r` attribute.

```
// A simple circle example.
svg.create('circle').set({ cx: 50, cy: 50, r: 25 });
```

In the next sketch, let's shift things up a gear with a `for` loop. We're going to play with the effect of layering semitransparent circles of different sizes over each other (shown in Figure 3-2). Copy our template folder again and rename it to `03-circle-overlay-loop` or something similar (the names of our folders don't really matter provided we maintain a modicum of organization).

Beneath where we defined our background, include the following code:

```
// Circle overlay loop.
for (let i = 1; i <= 6; i += 1) {

  // Vary the radius, and the two vertical centre points.
  let r = 50 * i;
  let cx = 500;
  let cy1 = 800 - r;
  let cy2 = 200 + r;
```

```
  // Create the blueish circle set.
  svg.create('circle').set({
    cx: cx, cy: cy1, r: r, fill: '#99eeff', fill_opacity: 0.1
  });

  // Create the greenish circle set.
  svg.create('circle').set({
    cx: cx, cy: cy2, r: r, fill: '#aaffee', fill_opacity: 0.1
  });
}

// Create a subtle outline.
svg.create('circle').set({
  cx: 500, cy: 500, r: 320, fill: 'none',
  stroke: '#aaffee', stroke_width: 2, stroke_opacity: 0.1
});
```

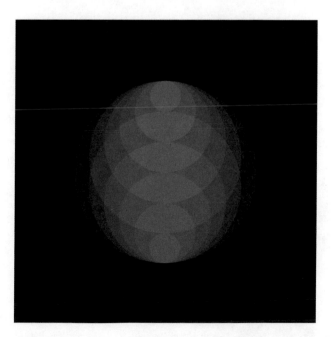

***Figure 3-2.*** *The result of our circle overlay loop*

What we've done here is vary the vertical position of the cy attribute and increase the radius r for two sets of circles each time the loop runs. The circle sets are differentiated by their color (slightly) and initial positions. A final circle outside the loop provides a subtle outline to frame the circle sets.

Ellipses are similar to circles but offer two radii attributes – rx and ry – instead of the single r. In the first generative sketch from Chapter 1, we saw the ellipse in action. Here's the relevant snippet:

```
// Create our ellipse.
let ellipse = svg.create('ellipse');
ellipse.set({
  cx: center,
  cy: center,
  rx: radiusX,
  ry: radiusY,
  ...
});
```

## Lines, Polylines, and Polygons

If you need to draw a simple straight line from one point to another, you'd use the line element. It requires two sets of coordinates: x1 and y1 to define the initial position and x2 and y2 to define the endpoint. It also requires the stroke to be defined (as it is a line after all).

```
// The humble line.
svg.create('line').set({
  x1: 10, y1: 10, x2: 90, y2: 90, stroke: '#333'
});
```

This is a good opportunity to showcase some other stroke-related attributes that can alter the appearance of a line. The first is `stroke-linecap`. This defines how the endpoints of a line behave. The default value, `butt`, limits the line length to its endpoints. A value of `round` will close off the line with a semi-circle at each end, whereas a value of `square` will close it off with – you guessed it – a square. Figure 3-3 shows the different values, with vertical lines on either side to delineate where the values come into effect.

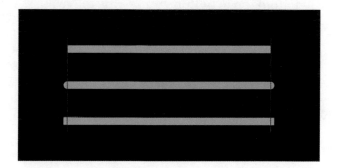

***Figure 3-3.***  *Values of butt, round, and square (top to bottom)*

The other attribute I want to highlight is `stroke-dasharray`. If, rather than a solid line, you would prefer a stroke consisting of dashes, this is what you would use. More specifically, the `stroke-dasharray` sets the pattern of dashes – and the gaps between them – with which to paint a stroke.

If we set a single value, say 20, that value will be used for the length of the dash and the length of the gap. If we set two values, the first is used for the dash and the second for the gap. If however we set three values, the first is used for the dash, the second for the gap, and the third for the next dash. The values are then cycled through again, creating a repeating pattern.

There isn't a strict upper limit on the amount of values you provide, so there is scope to get quite creative here.

```
// Setting an irregular stroke-dasharray.
svg.create('line').set({
  ...
  stroke_dasharray: 10 30 60
});
```

In Figure 3-4, from top to bottom, we see the following stroke-dasharray values (all relative to a viewBox width of 1000):

- 20

- 40 20

- 10 30 60

- 50 100 200 100

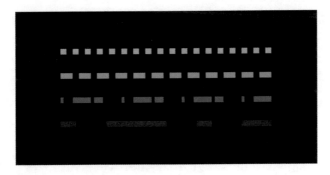

***Figure 3-4.*** *Various stroke-dasharray values*

If you want to connect one straight line to another, you'd use a polyline element. This takes a points array of space-separated (or comma-separated) values to define each x and y coordinate. The array of points needs to be converted to a string before being set as the attribute value. I show how to do this in the following example using the join() array method. The result is shown in Figure 3-5.

```
// An array of points.
let pointsArray = [
  100, 250, 250, 250, 285, 175, 325, 325, 390, 50, 450, 400,
  500, 200, 515, 250, 900, 250
];

// A polyline element, mimicking a heartbeat.
svg.create('polyline').set({
  points: pointsArray.join(' '),
  stroke: '#6df876',
  fill: 'none',
  stroke_width: 10,
  stroke_linecap: 'round',
  stroke_linejoin: 'round'
});
```

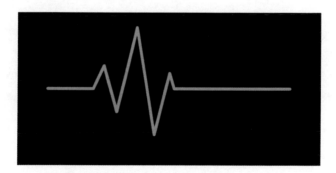

***Figure 3-5.***  *A polyline element in action*

I've also used the `stroke-linejoin` attribute in the preceding example; this defines the shape to use at point where each line meets the next.

A `polygon` element is similar to a `polyline` element but is used for closed shapes, that is, where the start and end points connect. In Figure 3-6, we see an arrangement of polygons that might be familiar to gamers of a particular platform.

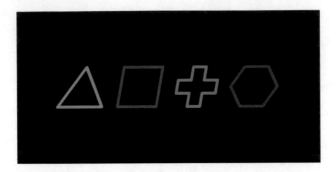

***Figure 3-6.*** *Polygons for the players*

Manually creating shapes with either the `polygon` or `polyline` elements isn't something we'll focus further on for now, as it can be quite tedious. There are better ways to generate shapes that we'll cover in a later chapter.

# Text and Titles

As SVG is a plain text format, it's no surprise that it supports textual elements. To create some text, we use the usual `svg.create()` method. At a minimum, we need to define the x and y coordinates of where we want it to appear (relative to the bottom left corner of the text's bounding box), its color, and its content.

```
// Creating text.
let text = svg.create('text').set({
  x: 20, y: 30, fill: 'white'
});
```

So how do we define the textual content if the content isn't itself an attribute? It's not a child node either, so creating a string and appending it wouldn't work. Instead, what we need to do is use the SvJs `content()` method.

```
// Using the content() method to insert text.
text.content('I have an unhealthy obsession with SVG.');
```

What if we wanted to get a bit more elaborate with our text and style them with some web fonts? There are a few ways we could do this, but I'll stick with the simplest and pull in some Google fonts via our HTML. Let's use this as the basis of a quick sketch; copy our 00-template folder and call it 04-chalkboard-gag.

If you've ever watched *The Simpsons*, you'll know that the beginning of most episodes features a chalkboard gag, where Bart is shown scrawling lines on a chalkboard as punishment for his errant behavior. One of my favorites is featured in the following sketch.

What we need to do first is include the following <link> in our HTML, so switch over to the index.html file and add the following line to the <head> section. This calls in a Google font called Mynerve, which has the handwritten look we're going for.

```
<link href="https://fonts.googleapis.com/css2?family=Mynerve
&display=swap"
rel="stylesheet">
```

If Bart had the option of running a for loop to minimize the repetitive nature of his punishment, I'm sure he would have taken it. Let's do this on his behalf (and cheat Skinner out of some satisfaction).

Add the following code below where we declare our background. Some points to note: we're calling the toUpperCase() string method to capitalize the content; this is a useful method to know, as is the related toLowerCase() method. The font_size of 52 is used to optimally fill the viewBox width, and incrementing the y position on each iteration by 80 is what pushes the lines down our chalkboard. We have enough space to do this 12 times, which is why we limit incrementation to below 960 (960 ÷ 80 = 12). Another iteration would overflow the viewport.

The output is shown in Figure 3-7.

```
// The line to use for the gag.
let line = '"Bart Bucks" are not legal tender.';
line = line.toUpperCase();
// Run a loop, creating 12 (960 / 80) lines of text.
for (let i = 0; i < 960; i += 80) {
  let text = svg.create('text');
  text.content(line);
  text.set({
    x: 20,
    y: 80 + i,
    fill: '#fff',
    font_size: 52,
    font_family: 'Mynerve'
  });
}
```

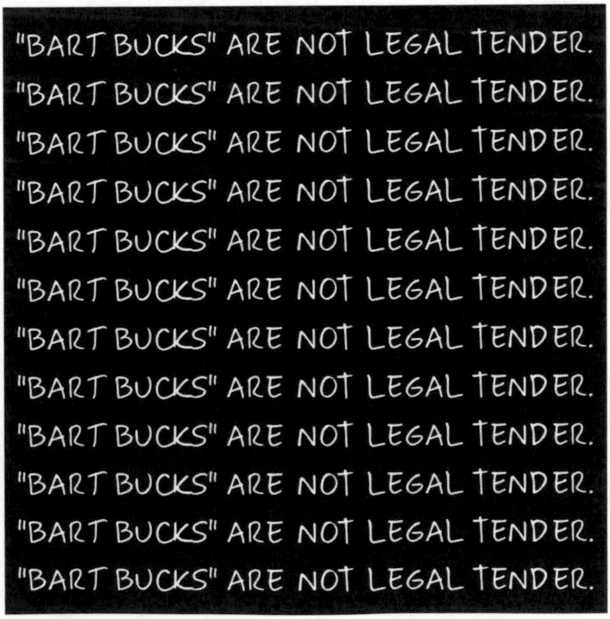

***Figure 3-7.*** *The "Bart Bucks" chalkboard gag*

Titles are another type of text we can use. Unlike a text element, a title element doesn't need to be positioned; it is intended to be nested within an element as a description. It works in the same way an HTML title attribute works; it helps with accessibility and appears as a tooltip on hover. It can be used to title the parent SVG element, or any of its child elements.

```
// Create a title for a circle element.
let circle = svg.create('circle');
let circleTitle = circle.create('title'); circleTitle.
content('I get around-round, I get around.');
```

A title element is suitable for shorter descriptions; for more extended descriptions, the desc element is recommended. This doesn't render and is purely for accessibility purposes, and is created in exactly the same way as a title element.

If you want to add extra information about the SVG file itself, the metadata element can be used. An example would be embedding RDF (Resource Description Framework) data, or application-specific data. You'll often see software like Inkscape or Illustrator embed their own metadata in this manner.

# Definitions

If we want to define a graphical or other container element for use in our SVG but don't want that element itself to appear (or if we want it to appear only when referenced), we would nest in within the defs element, which stands for definitions. The defs element can improve the overall accessibility of an SVG and also better help organize its content.

We'll rely on the functionality provided by the defs element in the upcoming sections on gradients, patterns, and other reusable elements.

```
// Defining a defs element.
let defs = svg.create('defs');
```

# Gradients

A gradient is a gradual transition from one color state to another. In SVG, gradients can support a multitude of these different color states (or "stops" as they're called). Most often, you'll see gradients of the two-stop variety, but occasionally you'll come across one boasting a rainbow-esque array of different colors. And speaking of rainbows, the sky itself is a great source of gradient inspiration (gradienspiration?). Think of the dim light at dusk where soft yellows transition to light blues, or the brilliant blaze of a sunset where purples, reds, and oranges collide.

Gradients can be of two varieties: linear (a color transition that proceeds from one area to another in a straight line) and radial (a color transition that emanates outward in all directions from a focal point).

How would we create such gradients in SvJs? It turns out it would be a very verbose process using just the `create()` method, and there's a couple of reasons for this:

- Gradients are defined as stand-alone elements within the `defs` section rather than treated as purely presentational element attributes. The upside of this is that a single gradient can be shared among multiple elements, but the downside is we've got a couple of extra steps to begin with.

- For each gradient color, a `stop` element must be defined and nested within the gradient element to define the color and its offset (or position). This adds another series of steps.

To remedy the aforementioned, SvJs offers a dedicated `createGradient()` method that significantly speeds up the process of constructing a gradient. Its syntax is as follows:

```
createGradient(id, type, colours, rotation)
```

With the first argument, we assign an id to the gradient so that it can be referenced or called upon later by an element. With the second argument, we specify the gradient type, that is, linear or radial. With the third argument, we pass in an array of color values. And with the final argument, we specify the angle of rotation, which is 45° by default (meaning it "shines" from the top left to the bottom right). This last argument is optional and is only applicable to gradients of the linear variety.

The createGradient() method can only be called by the parent SVG, as behind the scenes it checks whether a defs element is already defined within the SVG, and if not, it creates it and appends the gradient to it.

Here's how we might create a simple three-stop linear gradient and apply it to a rect element.

```
// Create the gradient with an id of 'grad'.
svg.createGradient('grad', 'linear', ['red', 'orange',
'yellow'], 90);

// Apply the gradient to the fill of the rect via a url
reference.
svg.create('rect').set({
  x: 0, y: 0, width: 400, height: 400, fill: 'url(#grad)'
});
```

As you can see, the shape we want the gradient applied to references the gradient id as an internal url. In the preceding example, we've applied it to the fill attribute, but it could also have been applied to the stroke.

In Figure 3-8, we see an example of three linear gradients and their radial equivalents. The first gradient has two color stops, the second has three, and the third has four. As you can see, it's easier to make linear gradients look smoother; with radial gradients, subtlety is always better, as transitions can seem relatively abrupt (or banded) compared to their linear counterparts.

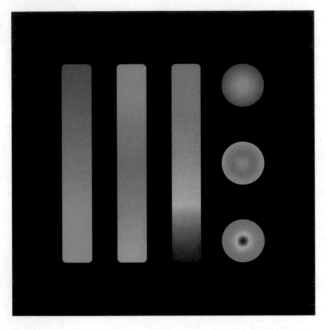

**Figure 3-8.**  *Linear gradients and their radial equivalents*

There are more ways to customize gradients that we won't get into here, but if you're interested, check out the MDN documentation for more on the gradient `spreadMethod` and varying the focal points of radial gradients.

# Patterns

Like gradients, patterns reside in the `defs` element to be referenced later rather than rendered directly. They have their own `viewport` (i.e., width and height) and optional `viewBox`, which can seem a little complicated at first, but it does allow for a greater degree of flexibility. Think of a `pattern` element as a miniature canvas to be replicated across a larger graphical element and these settings will make more sense.

To create a pattern, we can use the `createPattern()` shortcut method, which, as with the gradient method, automatically appends itself to a `defs` element and creates one if it doesn't exist. It also simplifies pattern creation in other ways under the hood that you don't have to worry about. It requires three arguments: the pattern `id`, the `width`, and the `height`.

To show how patterns work, we'll create a quick sketch – another optical illusion, but this time the focus won't be on the colors. Copy our `00-template` folder and rename it to `05-optical-illusion`.

In our `sketch.js` file below the code for the background, create a pattern with an `id` of 'illusion' and with a width of 100 and a height of 200.

```
// Create our pattern.
const pattern = svg.createPattern('illusion', 100, 200);
```

This simply initializes our pattern; we haven't placed anything within it yet, nor have we set up a shape to apply it to. We just have a pattern in the shape of a vertical rectangle.

In our first iteration of this sketch, I'll show you how a simple pattern gets applied to a shape. We'll get more elaborate with the pattern content afterward. Add the following code to our sketch:

```
// Create a white rectangle within the pattern.
pattern.create('rect').set({
  x: 10, y: 10, width: 80, height: 180, fill: '#eee'
});
```

Now that we have our simple pattern in place (consisting of a single white rectangle), it's time to apply it to a shape. For simplicity, let's apply it to another `rect` the full size of the SVG `viewBox`, like so:

```
// Apply our pattern to a rect the size of the viewBox.
svg.create('rect').set({
  x: 0, y: 0, width: 1000, height: 1000, fill: 'url(#illusion)'
});
```

You should now see something similar to Figure 3-9. Not especially interesting, but sufficient to showcase the basics.

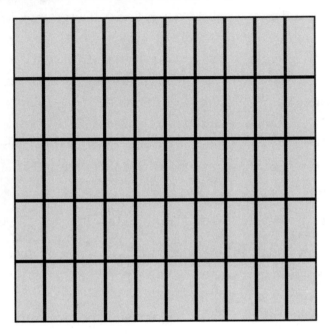

***Figure 3-9.***  *A basic pattern*

In the next few steps, we'll create our optical illusion. First, comment out the code that created the white rectangle pattern (but keep the shape it's applied to).

```
// Create our pattern.
const pattern = svg.createPattern('illusion', 100, 200);

// Create a white rectangle within the pattern.
// pattern.create('rect').set({
//   x: 5, y: 5, width: 90, height: 190, fill: '#eee'
// });

// We'll place our new code here.
```

```
// Apply our pattern to a rect the size of the viewBox.
svg.create('rect').set({
  x: 0, y: 0, width: 1000, height: 1000, fill: 'url(#illusion)'
});
```

To create the base of our optical illusion, we need a total of eight rectangles. Four of them will be white squares arranged in a particular order, and four will be thin gray rectangles used as separators. We'll use a couple of for loops to create these.

First, the white squares:

```
// Create 4 x white squares within the pattern.
for (let i = 0; i < 4; i += 1) {
  pattern.create('rect').set({
    x: (i === 3) ? 20: i * 20,
    y: i * 50,
    width: 50,
    height: 50,
    fill: '#eee'
  });
}
```

The width, height, and fill merely repeat themselves on each iteration; the only attributes we're varying are the x and y coordinates. To do this, we're using the changing value of the i iterator. The y coordinate increases by 50 on each run, which is simple enough. The expression defining the x position is a little more complicated. What we're saying here is that we want x to increase by 20 on each iteration, *except* for the final one (where i === 3). For this, we want to set it to 20.

If you view the pattern at this point, you should see an undulating array of squares. It's not an optical illusion yet; it looks more like rudimentary pixel art. To complete the illusion, we need our separators.

```
// Create 4 x thin grey rectangles to separate the squares.
for (let i = 0; i < 4; i += 1) {
  pattern.create('rect').set({
    x: 0,
    y: 45 + (i * 50),
      width: 100,
      height: 5,
      fill: '#666'
  });
}
```

Now when you hit save, you should see something like Figure 3-10.

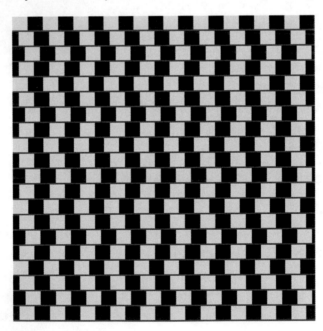

***Figure 3-10.*** *A repeating pattern creating an optical illusion*

If the illusion worked, the gray lines should appear slightly slanted, particularly those you're not directly focusing on. Hopefully this will give you some sense of the power of patterns! We've touched on the main points, but they can be customized extensively with further parameters if needed.

# Grouping and Reusing Elements

Grouping elements together can be done with the g element. There are a number of use cases for this. One, which applications like Inkscape have adopted, is to use the g element to support layer functionality. Another is to group elements together for the purposes of transformation (i.e., moving, rotating, or skewing multiple elements at once). And another is to simply group items together to better organize your SVG.

```
// Create a circle and add it to a group.
const circle = svg.create('circle');
const group = svg.create('g');
circle.addTo(group);
```

If you want to group elements together for later reuse (so that they are only displayed when referenced), you'd use the symbol element. Symbols, like patterns, can have their own viewport and viewBox. But they are called via the use element rather than applied to a fill or stroke.

```
// Create a symbol consisting of a circle and square.
const symbol = svg.create('symbol');
symbol.set({ id: 'mySymbol', width: 100, height: 100 });
symbol.create('circle').set({ ... });
symbol.create('rect').set({ ... });
```

```
// Using the symbol three times but varying its co-ordinates.
svg.create('use').set({ href: '#mySymbol', x: 0, y: 0 });
svg.create('use').set({ href: '#mySymbol', x: 200, y: 200 });
svg.create('use').set({ href: '#mySymbol', x: 400, y: 400 });
```

Symbols don't have quite the same appeal outside of a declarative context, so going forward we won't be relying on them for our imperative-based creations. But there's plenty more to unpack if you want to explore further on MDN.

# Summary

To recap, we've covered the following in this chapter:

- The core functions provided by the SvJs library

- How the SVG `viewBox` and `viewport` work

- Creating basic shapes like rectangles, circles, ellipses, polylines, and polygons

- Customizing `stroke` behavior and appearance

- Working with text and titles

- Creating gradients and patterns

- How definitions, groups, and symbols allow us to reuse elements and better structure our SVG

In the next chapter, we'll explore how we can combine regularity with randomness to create truly generative compositions.

# CHAPTER 4

# Randomness and Regularity

So far, all of our sketches (bar the first one) have lacked a certain ingredient usually considered foundational to the very genre of generative art: namely, randomness. When we surrender full control over the result of our sketches and leave certain elements to chance, it allows for variation, for exploration, and for *discovery*.

In this chapter, we'll learn how to randomize parameters like colors, sizes, and coordinates; how to randomly pick from predefined ranges and arrays; and how to work with different probability distributions. We'll also cover a popular generative technique that involves constructing regular grids and randomizing their contents. We'll then learn how to apply randomness to the construction of the grids themselves so that the underlying structure of our compositions can be varied.

## Analogue and Digital Randomness

Techniques to incorporate randomness into art began long before the digital age. As far back as the fifteenth century, Leonardo da Vinci suggested that artists take inspiration from sources rich in random and suggestive detail, such as the arbitrary forms found on the surface of stained stones and dirty walls. Artists like Max Ernst took such prompts

© David Matthew 2024
D. Matthew, *Generative Art with JavaScript and SVG*, Design Thinking,
https://doi.org/10.1007/979-8-8688-0086-3_4

quite literally; his frottage technique was borne of dropping paper at random on floorboards full of scrapes and scratches and making charcoal rubbings from the textures.

Contemporaries of Ernst, the early twentieth-century surrealists, also played with randomness. They developed a technique known as automatism, which aimed to eradicate full conscious control over an artwork's execution, allowing chance and the unconscious to act as the primary driving forces.

These examples, however, all draw upon the randomness found in the analogue world. In the more deterministic world of the digital, where ones and zeros reign, true randomness is harder to find. It must instead be simulated.

The good news is that this is more of an academic point than a practical obstacle. Simulated randomness (or pseudo-randomness as it's referred to in the field of computer science) is more than enough for our needs. And it's very easy to demonstrate this too, thanks to JavaScript's built-in `Math.random()` function. Typing the function into your browser console and hitting return should provide sufficient assurance that the 17-decimal floating-point number it throws back at you is unlikely to repeat itself anytime soon. Random enough, right?

```
Math.random();
-> 0.32846662956382255
```

The limitation of this function is that it only returns a number between 0 and 1. Granted, we can easily multiply the output by whatever factor we want, but what if we needed a number within a specific range? Or wanted to choose an item at random from an array?

# The SvJs Gen.random() Function

Thankfully the SvJs library comes armed with some extras: specifically, an optional module called Gen that contains a number of useful functions for generative artists. One of these is the Gen.random() function.

To load the Gen module, we need to add it to our import statement at the top of our sketches. Modify the template sketch to include this as the first line (replacing the previous import statement):

```
import { SvJs, Gen } from '../../node_modules/svjs/src/
index.js';
```

Now we can call Gen.random() and any of the other Gen methods (more of which we'll cover later). When called without any arguments, Gen.random() behaves just like Math.random(); it returns a floating-point number between 0 and 1.

```
Gen.random();
-> 0.5682831319665758
```

If, however, we supply some arguments, it suddenly becomes a lot more useful. Here are some examples:

```
// Return an integer between 50 and 100.
Gen.random(50, 100);
-> 87
```

```
// Return a floating point number between 10 and 20.
Gen.random(10, 20, true);
-> 17.98188644344106
```

```
// Return a random item from an array.
let rainbow = ['red', 'yellow', 'pink', 'green', 'purple',
'orange', 'blue'];
Gen.random(rainbow);
-> 'purple'
```

As you can see, if we provide two numbers, the `Gen.random()` function will treat them as the lower and upper thresholds of a range and return a number within that range. An integer is returned by default, but if we set the third argument to `true`, it will return a floating-point number. It will also return a floating-point number if we supply no arguments at all (as in our first example), or if the difference between the first and second arguments is less than or equal to one.

If we pass in an array as the sole argument, an item is randomly selected from that array. I purposely used colors in the example (apologies if the "Sing a Rainbow" song got stuck in your head), as this functionality is particularly useful when selecting colors from a predefined palette.

# Elements Everywhere All at Once

Let's create a sketch and put `Gen.random()` to work. Copy the `00-template` file as we usually do and rename it to something like `06-elements-everywhere`.

Below our background code, initialize a variable to store a random iteration count, which will determine how many times our `for` loop (which we'll set up after) will run.

```
let iterations = Gen.random(500, 1000);
```

Our `iterations` will be an integer anywhere between 500 and 1000. With that in place, let's write the loop. We'll keep it simple initially and just use it to create small circles. Each circle will be given a random position within the dimensions of the `viewBox` (0 to 1000), and its radius will be between 1 and 10. This should create an effect not too dissimilar to the spattering of paint (illustrated in Figure 4-1).

```
for (let i = 0; i < iterations; i += 1) {
  svg.create('circle').set({
    cx: Gen.random(0, 1000),
```

```
    cy: Gen.random(0, 1000),
    r: Gen.random(1, 10)
  });
}
```

***Figure 4-1.*** *A random spattering of circles*

# Varying Color and Opacity

At this point, we have colorless spatters randomly speckling the canvas. Let's change this up by varying the hue and opacity of the fill. We'll do this with the hsl() function, which is something we'll be drawing upon quite a lot. Its syntax is as follows:

```
hsl(hue saturation lightness / alpha)
```

The hue can be any number between 0 and 360. The saturation and lightness are percentage values, and the alpha component (which determines the opacity) can be either a percentage or a number between 0 and 1.

In our loop, add the following line below the radius (making sure to separate the lines with a comma):

```
fill: `hsl(${Gen.random(0, 360)} 80% 80% / ${Gen.
random(5, 40)}%)`
```

Now our speckles have come a little more to life (see Figure 4-2). But why stick to circles? Why not throw some other elements into the mix and make it look a little less like a cosmic ball pit? In the next version of the sketch, we'll do precisely that. The complexity will ramp up considerably, so we'll step through it slowly.

***Figure 4-2.*** *A more colorful spatter*

# Varying Element Selection

Below our `iterations` variable, create an array called `elements` and populate it with a `circle`, a `line`, and a `rect`:

```
let elements = ['circle', 'line', 'rect'];
```

Next, delete all the existing code in our `for` loop, and replace it with the following line that will pick a random element from the `elements` array defined previously.

```
// Pick a random element.
let element = Gen.random(elements);
```

In the next step, we'll initialize some variables with random values that we can later apply to our randomly selected element. In addition to our x, y, and `fill`, we'll also vary our `stroke` and `stroke-width`.

```
// Set up variables that we can use on any element.
let x = Gen.random(200, 800);
let y = Gen.random(200, 800);
let fill = `hsl(${Gen.random(120, 240)} 80% 80% / ${Gen.random(5, 40)}%)`;
let stroke = `hsl(${Gen.random(0, 120)} 80% 80% / ${Gen.random(5, 40)}%)`;
let strokeWidth = `${Gen.random(1, 3)}`;
```

You'll notice here that I've constrained the x and y variables to a range of 200 to 800, which ensures our shapes remain within that region and don't cover the entire canvas. This is so that we end up something that more closely resembles a composition than an explosion.

Next we'll set up a `props` variable (a commonly used shorthand for properties). The idea is that we set our element properties in accordance with the element chosen. Given that each element has its own distinct syntax for certain attributes (e.g., a `rect` has an x and y, but a circle has a cx and cy), we need to have a way of conditionally populating the props. There are a few ways we could approach this, but a switch statement lends itself particularly well to this situation. It allows us to populate the props variable on a case-by-case basis (quite literally, as you'll see).

```
// Initialise the properties variable.
let props;

// Populate the properties depending on the element chosen.
switch(element) {
  case 'circle':
    props = {
      cx: x, cy: y, r: Gen.random(1, 10),
      fill: fill, stroke: stroke, stroke_width: strokeWidth
    };
    break;
  case 'line':
    props = {
      x1: x, y1: y, x2: x + (Gen.random(-20, 20)),
      y2: y + (Gen.random(-20, 20)), stroke: stroke
    };
    break;
  case 'rect':
    props = {
      x: x, y: y, width: Gen.random(5, 25), height:
      Gen.random(5, 25),
      fill: fill, stroke: stroke, stroke_width: strokeWidth,
      transform: `rotate(${Gen.random(0, 360)} 500 500)`
    };
}
```

The one line here that perhaps calls for a little further explanation is the transform attribute included in the rect properties. This attribute can take either a translate, rotate, scale, or skew command as its argument, along with a transform value and two other values that represent the transform origin. The origin is a set of x and y coordinates that define the point relative to which the transform occurs. For example, in the case of the rotate command, we are randomly rotating the rect relative to 500 500, that is, the center of the viewBox.

We have one line left to include in the loop, right after our switch statement. This is the line that actually creates the element and applies the props to it.

```
// Create the element and set its properties.
svg.create(element).set(props);
```

When you run the sketch now, you should (hopefully) see something along the lines of Figure 4-3. Perhaps we weren't so successful in making it look less explosive (it looks like an eruption of confetti to me), but the different shapes and the addition of stroke values definitely add more in the way of variety and visual interest.

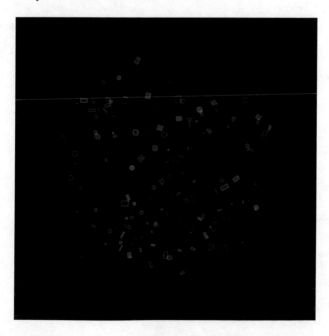

***Figure 4-3.***  *A confetti-like scattering of random elements*

# Regular Grids

Unrestrained randomness will only get us so far; we need techniques to tame and constrain it. One particularly prominent technique in the generative art world is to work with grids, which allow us to structure our randomness.

## The Nested For Loop

The nested for loop consists of one loop running within another. Because grids are comprised of columns (along the x axis) and rows (along the y axis), the nested for loop comes in very useful in their construction. What we'll typically do is start along the y axis and create our rows, and for each row, we move from left to right along the x axis, filling out each cell within the column. This movement mimics how computers have historically drawn pixel data to their displays; start at the top left, move across, and work your way down.

The outer loop will therefore be our y axis, moving down. For each iteration of the y axis, the inner (nested) loop will move across, populating the x axis.

```
// Example nested loop structure.
for (let y = 0; y < height; y += 1) {
  for (let x = 0; x < width; x += 1) {
    // Code goes here.
  }
}
```

Let's create a sketch to better illustrate this. Copy and rename the template folder, renaming it to 07-regular-grids. Below the background, we'll set up a group element to act as our grid container.

```
// Create our grid container group.
let grid = svg.create('g');
```

Now we'll run our `for` loop, appending a `rect` element to the `grid` on each iteration.

```
// A nested loop to visualise the grid.
for (let y = 0; y < 700; y += 50) {
  for (let x = 0; x < 700; x += 50) {
    grid.create('rect').set({
      x: x, y: y, width: 40, height: 40, fill: 'none',
      stroke: '#eee'
    });
  }
}
```

The values we've used here aren't especially meaningful; we could have chosen a different increment value, iteration count, width and height for the square, etc. We can tidy up these values later. What you will notice if you run `live-server` is that the grid is positioned off-center, to the top left (as our x and y values initialize at 0). We could adjust the x and y values until the grid lines up with the center of the `viewBox`, but that would involve some tedious trial and error and would need to be adjusted each time we altered the grid. Instead, let's use the built-in SvJs `moveTo()` method.

The `moveTo()` method moves a given element by its center point to a new position. The new position is passed in as an (x, y) coordinate pair. This method is especially useful on a group element (where the center point isn't straightforward to calculate) but can also be used as a more intuitive alternative to the `transform: translate(x y)` syntax.

SvJs also offers a related `getCentre()` method (which the `moveTo()` method also utilizes internally) to retrieve an element's center coordinates, returned as an `object` with x and y properties. This is useful when you want to position one element inside another.

After the loop, call the moveTo() method as follows:

```
// Centre the grid within the viewBox.
grid.moveTo(500, 500);
```

The grid should now line up nicely in the center of our viewBox, as shown in Figure 4-4.

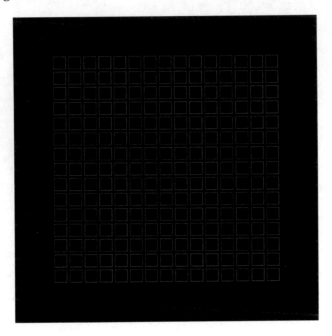

***Figure 4-4.***  *A regular, centered grid*

# A More Flexible Grid

So far we have hard-coded our grid values. By this, I mean we have used values directly to control the grid divisions, cell spacing, size, etc., rather than variables containing values. The latter approach allows for more flexibility.

Before our for loop, set and initialize the following variables. The values we'll use will reflect the grid we've already created; we'll alter these afterward.

```
// Set some grid-related variables.
let gridSize = 700;
let rows = 15;
let spacing = 5;
```

What we need next are variables that control the loop increment value and the size of each cell. These values, however, should be *derived* from those we've set previously, rather than worked out afresh each time we want to change the grid. With a little bit of basic math, here's how we'd do this:

```
let increment = gridSize / rows;
let cellSize = Math.abs(increment - spacing);
```

The Math.abs() function just ensures our cellSize is always a positive value, which can prevent errors if we go crazy with our rows and spacing values. Next, we need to incorporate these values into our loop. Adjust it as follows:

```
for (let y = 0; y < gridSize; y += increment) {
  for (let x = 0; x < gridSize; x += increment) {
    grid.create('rect').set({
      x: x, y: y, width: cellSize, height: cellSize,
      fill: 'none', stroke: '#eee',
    });
  }
}
```

Now we can freely adjust our grid variables, and the loop will respond accordingly. We could even randomize them and get a different grid on each refresh (as per Figure 4-5).

```
let gridSize = Gen.random(400, 800);
let rows = Gen.random(2, 20);
let spacing = Gen.random(5, 10);
```

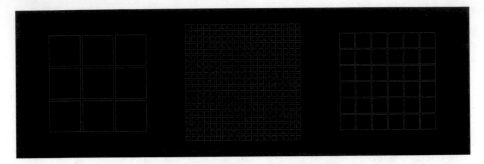

***Figure 4-5.*** *Variations of our regular grid*

# Clip Paths and Color Palettes

Now that we have our regular grid in place, we need to breathe some life into it. The changes we're going to make are significant enough to warrant a new iteration of our sketch, so if you'd prefer to keep what we've done so far as a template, save and copy the existing sketch folder and rename it to something like `08-colourful-grids`, which will give you a clue where we're taking this.

# Arrays of Colors

In our previous "Elements Everywhere" sketch, we used `Gen.random()` to generate our colors on the fly. But what if we wanted a particular color palette, or a collection of color palettes, so that we could randomly choose between them?

One popular approach is to store a pre-chosen palette as an array of color values, like so:

```
// Create a colour palette.
let palette = ['#5465FF', '#788BFF', '#9BB1FF', '#BFD7FF',
'#E2FDFF'];
```

There are many sites out there, too numerous to name, where you might stumble upon color palette inspiration. In fact, you might find it difficult to settle on a single palette, in which case it would make sense to save a selection of them and store them as arrays *within* another array. They would then become nested arrays, which are just arrays contained within other arrays. You might also see them referred to as 2D or multidimensional arrays.

Let's create a two-dimensional array containing three color palettes (illustrated in Figure 4-6). Beneath where we defined our initial grid group, include the following code (substituting in your own color palettes if you prefer):

```
// Create our colour palettes.
let palettes = [
    ['#5465FF', '#788BFF', '#9BB1FF', '#BFD7FF', '#E2FDFF'],
    ['#22577A', '#38A3A5', '#57CC99', '#80ED99', '#C7f9CC'],
    ['#4C5760', '#93A8AC', '#D7CEB2', '#A59E8C', '#66635B']
];
```

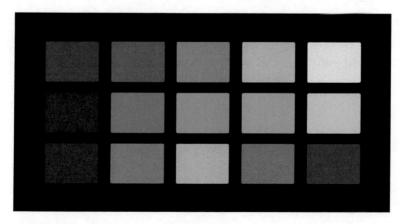

***Figure 4-6.*** *Our three colour palettes*

Next, we're going to randomly select one of these palettes and store it in a variable that we can call on later.

```
// Pick a random palette.
let pickedPalette = Gen.random(palettes);
```

Now on to our grid variables. You can leave this as they were from the last sketch, but I'm not going to randomize the gridSize or spacing this time, as I want to place the emphasis on other randomized elements of the sketch.

```
let gridSize = 600;
let rows = Gen.random(3, 10);
let spacing = 10;
let increment = gridSize / rows;
let cellSize = Math.abs(increment - spacing);
```

## Clipping Our Content

The next step in developing our grid-based composition will involve something called a clipPath. Essentially what a clipPath does is define the visible region of the shape it's applied to, in much the same way a scissors might define a cardboard cutout.

Instead of using a square to define our grid cells, we'll use a square-shaped clipPath. This way we can contain the content of our cells without them spilling out into adjacent cells. Let's step out our sketch for a moment to illustrate this. In Figure 4-7, we have a square-shaped rect that defines the clipPath, while the circle is the clipped element. On the right, you can see the effect of applying the clipPath to the circle.

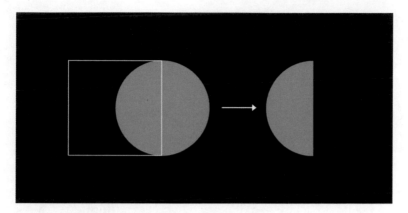

***Figure 4-7.*** *How a clipPath works*

A clipPath requires an id so that it can be referenced later. Nested within the clipPath element is the actual shape or path that will do the "clipping." Here's how we'd create something like the semi-circle example from Figure 4-7.

```
// Initialise the clipPath with an id.
let clip = svg.create('clipPath').set({ id: 'clip1' });

// Create the shape of the clipPath.
clip.create('rect').set({
  x: 0, y: 0, width: 100, height: 100, stroke: '#fff'
});

// Apply it to a circle via a call to its id.
svg.create('circle').set({
  cx: 100, cy: 50, r: 50, fill: '#80ffe6', clip_path:
  'url(#clip1)'
});
```

As you can see, the `clipPath` is called via its `id`, treated as an internal `url` reference, much like gradients and patterns. Let's get back to our sketch now and apply this same logic within our loop. First, create the nested loop as we did before:

```
for (let y = 0; y < gridSize; y += increment) {
  for (let x = 0; x < gridSize; x += increment) {
  }
}
```

Next, create the `clipPath`. We need to create a unique `id` for each instance, so we can't pass in a static string as we did previously – otherwise, the `id` would be duplicated on each loop iteration. Instead what we can do is use the `x` and `y` iterator variables to generate a dynamic string, using template literal syntax like so:

```
// Create our clip path with a unique id.
let clip = svg.create('clipPath').set({ id: `${x}${y}` });
```

Now we can create the actual shape of the `clipPath`. We'll keep it straightforward and make it square, that is, a `rect` with a `width` and `height` equal to our `cellSize`.

```
// Create the clip path shape.
clip.create('rect').set({
  x: x, y: y, width: cellSize, height: cellSize
});
```

With the `clipPath` in place, we need to decide what to put into it. Here's where we can get creative! There are four corners of each cell, so what we'll do is randomly center a group of circles at any one of these four positions. The coordinates of these positions are determined by the current x and y values, along with the `cellSize`. Here's how we'd calculate these positions and choose one of them at random:

```
// Define our possible positions.
let positions = [
  [x, y], // top left
  [x + cellSize, y], // top right
  [x + cellSize, y + cellSize], // bottom right
  [x, y + cellSize] // bottom left
];

// Pick a random position.
let pickedPosition = Gen.random(positions);
```

Now, to create the `circle` group. This will involve a third loop (so a loop within a loop within a loop – loopception if you will), where we will create five circles radiating out from a randomly chosen center point. And let's not forget about our palette picked out earlier; the fill of each circle will be colored accordingly.

```
// Create a group for our circles.
let circles = grid.create('g');

// Create the circles, applying the picked position and palette.
for (let i = 0; i < 5; i += 1) {
  circles.create('circle').set({
    cx: pickedPosition[0],
    cy: pickedPosition[1],
    r: cellSize - (i * (cellSize / 5)), // this took a bit of
                                        tweaking
    fill: pickedPalette[i]
  });
}
```

We have a couple more steps to go. We haven't actually *applied* the `clipPath` to anything yet, so if we were to run our sketch at this point, we'd just see a fairly cluttered overlap of circles. We'll fix this by applying the clipPath to the circle group rather than the circles themselves. And as the last step within the loop, we'll create a square border to frame each cell, just to give things a little more definition.

```
// Apply the clip path to the circle group.
circles.set({
  clip_path: `url(#${clip.get('id')})`
});

// Create a square to frame the cell.
grid.create('rect').set({
  x: x, y: y, width: cellSize, height: cellSize,
  fill: 'none', stroke: '#eee',
});
```

Now, outside the loop, center our grid as we've done before.

```
// Centre the grid within the viewBox.
grid.moveTo(500, 500);
```

And voila! You should now see some variations similar to those of Figure 4-8. (As an aside, if you find that the grid isn't always centering properly, that's because the grid's bounding box includes the invisible clipped content, which won't always arrange itself symmetrically around the grid.)

***Figure 4-8.*** *Colorful clip path grid patterns*

# Choice and Chance

What if we were to bring an element of chance into choosing whether or not to populate a given cell in our grid? This can lead to a less rigid-looking composition – which isn't necessarily better, but it can offer more in the way of variety.

## The SvJs Gen.chance( ) Function

When we talk about probability, what we're usually trying to establish are the chances, or the odds, of something occurring. This something will either happen or it won't, so what we want is a binary response – or boolean – to tell us yes or no, win or lose. Will your horse Victor Vector give you a payout at the races today? Given the odds are 7 to 2, there's a 22% chance of some winnings $(2 / (7 + 2) \times 100 = 22.22)$.

How could we work this kind of logic into our compositions? It's actually quite simple to do with plain JavaScript and `Math.random()`, but SvJs offers a more intuitive, less verbose alternative with its `Gen.chance()` function.

By default (i.e., without any arguments), `Gen.chance()` returns either `true` or `false` based on odds of 50/50, or 50%. If we supply a single argument, it's interpreted as a percentage.

```
// The below returns true 60% of the time.
Gen.chance(60);
```

If two numbers are supplied, the arguments are interpreted as odds. This can be useful if you prefer thinking of probabilities more in terms of placing a bet at a bookie than calculating a precise percentage value (which is actually done for you under the hood).

```
// There is a 7 to 2 chance of this returning true.
Gen.chance(7, 2);
```

# Chance in Action

Let's create a new sketch, using Gen.chance() to determine whether or not the cells within our grid get populated with content. Copy the 08-colourful-grids folder and rename it to 09-chance, and then remove all content from the inner loop (leaving you with an empty nested for loop). Next, replace the palettes array and pickedPalette variable with a randomly generated hue.

```
// Pick a random hue.
let hue = Gen.random(0, 360);
```

You can leave the grid-related variables as they are, or tweak them if you prefer. Next, *between* the x and y loops (so within the first loop but before the second), increment the hue like so:

```
// A nested loop to create the grid.
for (let y = 0; y < gridSize; y += increment) {

  // Increment the hue relative to the rows, keeping it within
    0 and 360.
  hue = (hue >= 360) ? (hue - 360) + (120 / rows) : hue + (120
  / rows);

  for (let x = 0; x < gridSize; x += increment) {
  ...
```

This might seem like an overly complex way of increasing the hue value, but really it's just doing two things: first, it's ensuring the hue value doesn't stray out of bounds (i.e., beyond 360), and second, it's incrementing the hue value relative to the number of rows. This is so that sketch variations with a lower row count have a higher increment value, and those with a higher row count have a lower increment value, resulting in greater color consistency overall.

Inside the x loop is where we'll actually use Gen.chance(). Used as a condition inside an if statement, we can conditionally fire a third loop based on the result it returns. This loop will create random line elements inside each cell, but only if the cell is activated by the Gen.chance() function. We'll set the actual probability to 60%.

```
// Run the loop based on chance.
if (Gen.chance(60)) {
  for (let i = 0; i < cellSize; i += 1) {
    grid.create('line').set({
      x1: Gen.random(x, x + cellSize),
      y1: Gen.random(y, y + cellSize),
      x2: Gen.random(x, x + cellSize),
      y2: Gen.random(y, y + cellSize),
      stroke: `hsl(${hue} 80% 80% / 0.33)`
    });
  }
}
```

This should result in gradiented tetris-like arrangements, similar to Figure 4-9.

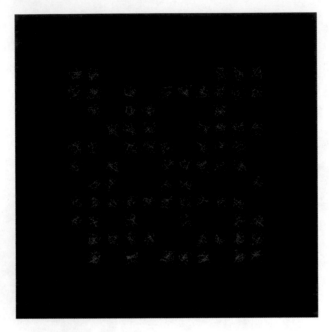

***Figure 4-9.***  *Gen.chance() in action*

# Probability Distributions

Probability distributions describe how numbers are spread out (or distributed) over a given range. Unless you've studied statistics in one form or another, you may not be too familiar with the term. And if the mere mention of statistics causes you to break out in a cold sweat, don't worry – we won't be delving into the underlying mathematics. We've actually been using a particular kind of probability distribution already but just haven't attached the name to it.

## Uniform Distribution

The Gen.random() function is an example of *uniform* distribution, where every number within the range has an equal chance of being chosen. In other words, there are no biases or tendencies hiding with the

Gen.random() function (or indeed, the Math.random() on which it is based) that make it more likely that a certain subset of numbers within the range will be selected.

In Figure 4-10, we can see uniform distribution visualized as the variation of the x coordinate in the placement of 1000 vertical lines. The lines are all scattered with equal chance of appearing anywhere along the x axis.

***Figure 4-10.***  *Uniform distribution of vertical lines*

## Gaussian Distribution

In real-life measurements (i.e., those outside the binary world of ones and zeros), uniform distribution isn't actually that common. Far more prevalent is something called *Gaussian* distribution, where the majority of values cluster toward a midpoint and drop off either side of this. It is also known as normal distribution, and when graphed, it forms a bell-shaped curve. Visualized as a series of vertical lines, it looks like Figure 4-11.

***Figure 4-11.***  *Gaussian distribution of vertical lines*

The midpoint around which most values accumulate is known as the mean, and the degree to which they drop off, or deviate, from this mean is known as sigma, or the standard deviation.

SvJs comes with a function called Gen.gaussian() that returns a random number that adheres to a Gaussian distribution. With no arguments, it will return values between approximately -3 and +3, with a mean of 0 and a standard deviation of 1. What this means in practice is that

- 68% of values will be within -1 and 1 (the standard deviation)

- 95% of values will be within -2 and 2

- 99% of values will be within -3 and 3

By supplying arguments to Gen.gaussian(), we can modify the mean and standard deviation.

```
// Adjusting the mean and standard deviation to 10 and 2
respectively.
Gen.gaussian(10, 2);
```

In the preceding example, adjusting the mean to 10 and standard deviation to 2 would translate to 68% of values falling within -2 and +2 of the mean (so between 8 and 12), 95% falling between 6 and 14, and more than 99% falling between 4 and 16. Strictly speaking, the values of a Gaussian distribution aren't bounded, so there may be occasional extreme outliers. If, for example, you wanted to make sure you kept the results to within a factor of 3 either side of the standard deviation, you could use the Gen.constrain() function to bound the results like so:

```
// Bounding the results of Gen.gaussian() to within -3 and +3.
let gaussian = Gen.gaussian(0, 1);
let constrainedGaussian = Gen.constrain(gaussian, -3, 3);
```

Let's move on and create a quick sketch to illustrate how we could use the results returned from Gen.gaussian() to map x and y coordinates across our viewBox. Copy our template and call it something like

10-gaussian-dist. In the usual place below our background, initialize a loop that will run 10,000 times (yep, that's a lot!), and inside it, generate a couple of Gaussian coordinates.

```
// Run a loop 10,000 times.
for (let i = 0; i < 10000; i += 1) {

  // Generate x and y co-ordinates with a gaussian distribution.
  let gaussianX = Gen.gaussian(500, 150);
  let gaussianY = Gen.gaussian(500, 150);
}
```

The coordinates are based around the center of the viewBox (i.e., 500), with a standard deviation of 150. Next, and still within the loop, create our lines, basing them on our Gaussian coordinates and adding a bit of randomization to their endpoints.

```
// Create the lines based on the gaussian co-ordinates.
svg.create('line').set({
  x1: gaussianX,
  y1: gaussianY,
  x2: gaussianX + Gen.random(-10, 10),
  y2: gaussianY + Gen.random(-10, 10),
  stroke: `hsl(${Gen.random(150, 270)} 80% 80% / 0.8)`
});
```

You could stop here and see the circular pattern that emerges, but I added another little loop (after the first one, not within it) to subtly emphasize the shape of the distribution with a series of fading circular strokes.

```
// Create a series of circles to frame the distribution.
for (let i = 0; i < 10; i += 1) {
  svg.create('circle').set({
    cx: 500, cy: 500, r: 25 + (i * 25), fill: 'none',
```

```
    stroke: `hsl(0 0% 0% / ${0.25 - (i / 50)})`, stroke_
    width: 15
  });
}
```

After this, you should end up with something similar to Figure 4-12.

***Figure 4-12.***  *Using Gen.gaussian to position 10,000 lines*

In terms of the generated markup, it's quite a heavy piece compared to anything we've done previously (10,000 elements will do that). This can adversely impact render performance and also means a bigger SVG file if you copy it from the HTML. One easy way to get the size down somewhat is to set the third argument to false in each instance of the Gen.gaussian() function. Like Gen.random(), Gen.gaussian() accepts a third argument that determines whether it returns a float (more accurate but with a lot of digits) or an integer (whole number). Dealing in whole numbers decreases the generated markup by roughly a factor of two in this case.

# Pareto Distribution

Pareto distribution, also known as the Pareto Principle or the 80-20 rule (illustrated in Figure 4-13), is the final probability pattern we'll cover. It is named after an Italian economist who famously observed that just 20% of a society's population controlled 80% of its wealth. This was the 1890's mind, so had Pareto made the same observations today, we might be discussing the 99-1 rule! Be that as it may, the basic idea remains the same: there is a lot with a little and a little with a lot.

***Figure 4-13.*** *Pareto distribution of vertical lines*

This can be useful in generative art to achieve a balance of differently sized elements. We'll use this in our next sketch to create a pseudo-cityscape called Porto Pareto, where the size of the city's buildings will be varied using the SvJs Gen.pareto() function. This function takes two arguments; the first defines the minimum number in the range to be returned, and the second defines whether this number will be a float or integer.

```
// Return a pareto-distributed integer, not less than 20.
Gen.pareto(20, false);
-> 32
```

Copy the template folder and name it 11-porto-pareto, and below the background, create a group that will contain our cityscape.

```
// Create a group for our generative city.
let portoPareto = svg.create('g');
```

The cityscape will have three main elements: the sky, the river (or port), and the buildings. The sky and river will both be simple `rect` elements with gradients; we'll create these first.

```
// Create the sky gradient.
svg.createGradient('sky', 'linear', ['#f58b10', '#d21263',
'#940c5e', '#25226c'],
90);

// Create the sky and apply the gradient.
portoPareto.create('rect').set({
  x: 150, y: 150, width: 700, height: 400, fill: 'url(#sky)'
});

// Create the river gradient.
svg.createGradient('river', 'linear', ['#80e5ff10',
'#70b566'], 90);

// Create the river and apply the gradient.
portoPareto.create('rect').set({
  x: 150, y: 555, width: 700, height: 295, fill: 'url(#river)'
});
```

Hopefully there won't have been any surprises in the aforementioned. Next up, we'll deal out some Pareto distribution and create our buildings. In the following loop, there's one line in particular I want to unpack, and this is where we set the height using the `Gen.constrain()` function. Without it, our Pareto distribution would generate some dizzyingly high buildings that would extend well beyond the canvas limits. However, using `Gen.constrain()` alone with a set upper limit leads to a clipped effect on the highest buildings, so to even this out, I've added in a `Gen.random()` function to vary the upper limit.

```
// A loop for our generative cityscape.
for (let i = 0; i < 60; i += 1) {
  // Get a pareto distribution with a min height of 20.
  let pareto = Gen.pareto(20);

  // Constrain the height, and slightly randomise the upper limit.
  let height = Gen.constrain(pareto, 20, Gen.random(150, 200));

  // Create our buildings.
  portoPareto.create('line').set({
    x1: 150 + (i * 12), y1: 550,
    x2: 150 + (i * 12), y2: 550 - height,
    stroke: '#181818', stroke_width: 8
  });
}
```

We now have our cityscape in place, but we're not done yet. It's quite flat-looking, and I'd like it to be framed within a circle and for the colors to look like they're emanating outward. To achieve this, I'm going to use something called a mask.

# Masking Our Content

A mask is very similar to a clipPath, except that it allows for degrees of transparency. A clipPath is an all-or-nothing affair; you're either inside or outside the bounds of the shape that defines it. With a mask, you can fade content in or out depending on the brightness or luminance of the shape. For this reason, it's most straightforward to use black and white when creating masks. White (#ffffff) translates to a fully transparent region, whereas black (#000000) translates to a fully opaque region.

In Figure 4-14, the triangle is the mask shape, and the result of applying it to the rect is shown on the right.

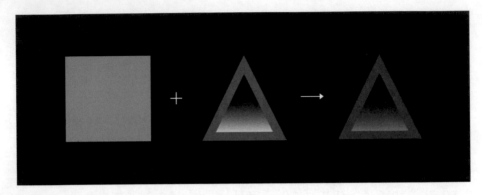

***Figure 4-14.*** *How masks work*

As with a clipPath, the mask element requires an id and is applied to another element via a url reference to this id. What we're going to do is create a mask with a circle shape, and the fill of this circle will contain a radial gradient. We'll then apply it to the portoPareto group we created earlier.

```
// Create a radial gradient.
svg.createGradient('radialGrad', 'radial', ['#ffffff',
'#ffffff60']);
```

```
// Create a mask, and inside it create the circle with the
radial gradient.
let mask = svg.create('mask').set({ id: 'mask' });
mask.create('circle').set({
  cx: 500, cy: 500, r: 325, fill: 'url(#radialGrad)',
});
```

```
// Apply the mask to the group.
portoPareto.set({ mask: 'url(#mask)' });
```

You should now see the cityscape cut out in the shape of this circle, with the edges slightly fading out. As a final step, I've added in a gradiented circular stroke to frame the content a little more clearly.

```
// Create a linear gradient for our circular frame.
svg.createGradient('strokeGrad', 'linear', ['#eeeeee',
'#eeeeee15']);

// Create the frame and apply the gradient.
svg.create('circle').set({
  cx: 500, cy: 500, r: 345, fill: 'none',
  stroke: 'url(#strokeGrad)', stroke_width: 2.5
});
```

A variation of the result is shown in Figure 4-15.

***Figure 4-15.*** *Our Porto Pareto cityscape*

# Summary

In this chapter, we've covered the following:

- Randomizing coordinates, colors, element dimensions, and more

- How to randomly pick items from single and two-dimensional arrays

- Regular grid construction with nested for loops

- How to use clipPaths and masks

- Using chance as a way to trigger element creation

- How to work with Gaussian and Pareto probability distributions

In the next chapter, we'll learn how to use noise to add a more organic kind of randomness to our compositions.

# CHAPTER 5

# The Need for Noise

In this chapter, we'll be covering the limitations of the random functions
we've utilized thus far and how these limitations can be addressed by
using the SvJs `Noise` module. We'll be exploring what noise is and the
uses to which it can be put, and by the end, we'll have added a significant
technique to our generative arsenal.

## Random Limits

Sometimes randomness is just too, well ... random. Even when we shape
randomized values with probability distributions and constrain them
within structured patterns, the variance between consecutive values
invariably has that characteristic "staccato" feel. In other words, the values
will always be somewhat jumpy and jittery when looked at side by side.
You won't see a smooth progression from one value to another.

 Don't get me wrong – this is often what we want, and it's what random
functions are designed to do. But it can be tricky to create anything that has
an organic quality to it with randomness alone. For this, we need noise.

## Making Noise

In 1997, Ken Perlin won an Oscar. What made this award unprecedented
was that Perlin wasn't an actor, director, or soundtrack composer, but
a programmer. For the movie *TRON*, released in 1982, Perlin had been

© David Matthew 2024
D. Matthew, *Generative Art with JavaScript and SVG*, Design Thinking,
https://doi.org/10.1007/979-8-8688-0086-3_5

tasked with the development of procedural textures that would make 3D objects look more natural (i.e., organic), and the algorithm he devised, named Perlin noise, has since become ubiquitous in the world of computer graphics. You'll find implementations in image editors like GIMP and Photoshop, in vector editors like Inkscape and Illustrator, in 3D graphics packages like Blender, and in countless video games down through the ages. Minecraft is a great example; those infinite blocky terrains where players mine for resources use height maps generated by Perlin noise to determine their various peaks and troughs.

So Perlin noise is everywhere in the graphical domain. But what exactly is it?

## Noise Explained

Technically, noise functions do produce random numbers, but they do so in a smoothly ordered fashion, and this is what makes the difference. In Figure 5-1, the height of the white lines is randomized using a Perlin noise variable. This is an example of one-dimensional noise, that is, noise values that operate along a single axis.

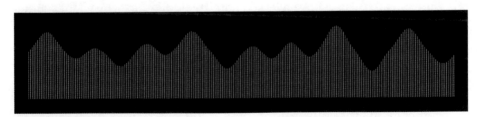

***Figure 5-1.***  *A one-dimensional representation of Perlin noise values*

Noise is by nature multidimensional; Perlin originally designed it for 3D spaces, and there are four-dimensional implementations out there too, but with SVG being a two-dimensional medium, I'll be sticking to the x and y axes. The particular algorithm Perlin developed works by blending randomized values in a gradiented fashion over a given area. This area, or space, is more notional than actual; the noise values don't exist on an actual plane or separate canvas, but rather in an abstract (and infinite) space that we can retrieve values from.

For example, fetching a noise value at the conceptual coordinates of (15, 20) would give us some value between -1 and 1. And when we slowly traverse through this noise space to reach an adjoining coordinate, say (16, 21), we get a series of smoothly varied values we can work with. And it's what we can do with those values that make noise interesting from an aesthetic perspective.

In Figure 5-2, we can see noise represented in two dimensions using the full area of a canvas. This example is actually pixel based rather than vector based, chosen because it's perhaps the best way to visually grasp the notion of a noise space. Here, the alpha component of each pixel is varied according to the corresponding noise value, creating a cloud-like formation. You can immediately see why it would be useful for creating textures.

*Figure 5-2.* *A two-dimensional representation of Perlin noise values*

## The SvJs Noise Module

The SvJs library comes with its own implementation of noise, designed
to be simple to use and to have as light a footprint as possible. It resides
in its own module, so like the Gen module, we have to import it before we
can use it.

```
import { Noise } from '../../node_modules/svjs/src/index.js';
```

Unlike Gen, which is a collection of functions, the Noise module is class
based, so we first need to instantiate it.

```
// Create an instance of the Noise class.
let noise = new Noise();
```

The class has a single method called get() that accepts an x coordinate and optional y coordinate as arguments and returns the value at that point in the noise space.

```
let noiseValue = noise.get(noiseX, noiseY);
```

That noiseValue won't be much use to us as a static value; what we need to do is gradually modify it by traversing the noise space. We do this by incrementing the noiseX and/or noiseY coordinates. Here's how this might look within a loop:

```
// Initialise our noise instance and noise co-ordinates first.
let noise = new Noise();
let noiseX = 15, noiseY = 20;

// Run the loop, slowly incrementing the co-ordinates to modify
the value.
for (let i = 0; i < 1000; i += 1) {
  let noiseValue = noise.get(noiseX, noiseY);
  ... // Do something with noiseValue

  noiseX += 0.003;
  noiseY += 0.003;

}
```

As you can see, we define the initial noiseX and noiseY coordinates outside the loop, use them to fetch a noiseValue within it, and then before the loop runs again, increment the coordinates by a very small amount. This amount we might refer to as the noise speed or rate of change. It's important when working with noise that this rate of change is minimal; comparatively large leaps (e.g., by whole numbers) won't yield usable results.

# Into the Noise Matrix

Let's copy our template and set up a new sketch folder called `12-noise-matrix`, to show how noise can be used to alter color values within a grid. At the top of our `sketch.js` file, add in the `Noise` module to our import statement like so:

```
import { SvJs, Gen, Noise } from '../../node_modules/svjs/src/index.js';
```

Next, we're going to shorten the expression that calculates the `svgSize` (and thus the dimensions of our `viewport`). Instead of the ternary operator, we can actually use the `Math.min()` function, which returns the smallest of two or more values. If you remember, all we want to do is set the `svgSize` to whichever of the window's `innerWidth` or `innerHeight` is smallest, and `Math.min()` does this in the most succinct manner. A small tweak to be sure, but one that hints at the many uses of JavaScript's built-in Math module.

```
const svgSize = Math.min(window.innerWidth, window.innerHeight);
```

I'd recommend applying this tweak to our base template too.

# A Noisy Grid

For this composition, we'll be using a familiar technique: we'll be setting up a grid, and this grid will act as our matrix (a matrix is, after all, just a grid of values). And the matrix we'll be creating in this sketch will mimic the one from the movie of the same name. We'll be populating the grid with ones and zeros, and the color of these digits will be modulated by noise to achieve that cascading, desaturated effect.

Create an instance of the noise class, and then initialize three further variables. Two will take care of our noise x and y coordinates, and in the third, we'll store the noise speed that will determine the rate at which we'll increment the noise coordinates.

```
// Create our noise, the noise x and y co-ordinates, and
noise speed.
let noise = new Noise();
let nX = 0, nY = 0;
let noiseSpeed = 0.5;
```

The next block of code should hopefully look familiar. We're setting some grid-related variables, and this time we'll omit the spacing and cellSize variables we used in previous sketches and set the gridSize to cover the entire viewBox.

```
// Set some grid-related variables.
let noiseGrid = svg.create('g');
let gridSize = 1000;
let rows = 80;
let increment = gridSize / rows;
```

Next comes our loop. Instead of starting with the y coordinate in the outer loop, we're going to start with the x coordinate. What this will do is construct our grid from top to bottom and then left to right. In other words, we'll fill out our columns first rather than the rows, which will allow our noise values to flow in a downward motion.

Within the loop, we'll fetch our noise value using the noise.get() method, passing in the nX and nY values we initialized earlier.

```
// Create the noise matrix.
for (let x = 0; x < gridSize; x += increment) {
  for (let y = 0; y < gridSize; y += increment) {
```

```
  // Fetch the noise value.
  let noiseValue = noise.get(nX, nY);

 }
}
```

Next, let's create the actual text content. We want a series of ones and zeros to fill the grid, with a 50% chance of either digit being chosen. As we learned in the last chapter, the `Gen.chance()` function is the simplest way to do this, combined with a ternary operator.

```
// Create text displaying either 0 or 1 (50% chance).
let text = noiseGrid.create('text');
text.content(Gen.chance() ? '1' : '0');
```

Now we need to set the position of the digit with respect to the x and y loop iterator values and set the intensity of the fill color (i.e., the lightness component of the `hsl()` function) with the `noiseValue` variable. We should also set a font size and font family while we're at it.

```
text.set({
  x: x, y: y,
  font_size: 16,
  font_family: 'serif',
  fill: `hsl(120 20% ${noiseValue}%)`
});
```

And before we close out our loop, we'll want to increment our nX and nY values with the `noiseSpeed` variable.

```
nX += noiseSpeed;
nY += noiseSpeed;
```

To finish off the sketch, outside the loop, call the moveTo() function to shift the grid to the center of the canvas.

```
// Centre the grid within the viewBox.
noiseGrid.moveTo(500, 500);
```

You should now see a grid of zeros and ones when you run your sketch. But ... they're all black. The color lightness isn't visibly changing, even though we're using our noiseValue to modify it. What's going on here?

If you inspect some of the text elements in the browser console, you'll see something like the following:

```
<text x="860" y="960" font-size="16" font-family='serif'
fill="hsl(120 20%
-0.11888951723051341%)">0</text>
<text x="860" y="980" font-size="16" font-family='serif'
fill="hsl(120 20%
-0.06168012594419729%)">1</text>
<text x="880" y="0" font-size="16" font-family='serif'
fill="hsl(120 20%
0.061791625695004807%)">0</text>
<text x="880" y="20" font-size="16" font-family='serif'
fill="hsl(120 20%
0.1202821001266494%)">1</text>
```

The point to note here is that when we call the noise.get() method, the value returned is a float between -1 and 1 (with some occasional outliers). The lightness component of the hsl() function, however, should have values between 0 and 100%, so in its raw state, the noise value isn't very useful here. How might we fix this? Couldn't we just multiply it by a factor of 100? We could, but we'd then have an equal amount of numbers in the negative range. And if we tried to remedy this with Math.abs() to force the negative numbers into a positive range, that would destroy the very raison d'être of noise – its smoothly transitioning values. So what's the solution?

# Mapping the Noise Values

This is actually a common challenge in generative art – mapping a series of values from one range to another. Thankfully the Gen module comes equipped with a function that does just this: Gen.map().

The function requires five arguments, with an optional sixth: the first is the value to be mapped to the new range, the second and third arguments define the lower and upper bounds of the existing range, and the fourth and fifth arguments define the lower and upper bounds of the range to which we want our value mapped. The final sixth argument specifies whether a float should be returned. In common with other Gen functions like gaussian and pareto, this is set to true by default, and setting it to false rounds the result to the nearest integer. The following is an example:

```
// Map a number (5) from one range (0, 10) to another (0, 100).
let num = 5;
num = Gen.map(num, 0, 10, 0, 100);
console.log(num);
-> 50
```

If we apply the Gen.map() function to our noiseValue variable, we can retrieve a more usable value. We could assign this new mapped value to a new variable, or as the preceding example shows us, we can simply reassign the original variable.

```
// Fetch the noise value.
let noiseValue = noise.get(nX, nY);

// Map the noise value to a useful range.
noiseValue = Gen.map(noiseValue, -1, 1, 0, 100, false);
```

Once you've done this, you should see some color injected into our matrix (as per Figure 5-3). Enough we hope to get an appreciative nod from Neo.

**Figure 5-3.** *That chunk of the matrix that tastes like chicken*

It's worth noting that when using a generic font-family like serif, you essentially let the operating system decide which default font to render. For this reason, what you see may differ slightly from Figure 5-3.

## Optimize with Style

We could leave it there and make no further changes to the sketch, but there's one little niggle I can't leave alone. In total, we have 2,500 text elements in this sketch, and for each of these elements, the font-size and font-family attributes remain static throughout. This seems quite wasteful.

```
<text x="740" y="200" font-size="16" font-family="serif"
fill="hsl(120 20%
50%)">1</text>
```

What we can do is first remove the font attributes set within the loop so that the `text.set()` method looks like the following:

```
text.set({
  x: x, y: y, fill: `hsl(120 20% ${noiseValue}%)`
});
```

Then we can create a `style` element and within it, target all our text elements at once. Near the top of our sketch, after the parent SVG declaration, include the following code:

```
// Set some text styling.
svg.create('style').content(`
  text {
    font-size: 16px;
    font-family: serif;
  }
`);
```

Note the use of backticks here; this allows us to indent our code just as we would with normal CSS. What this CSS does is apply the `font-size` and `font-family` to each of our `text` elements, avoiding the use of repetitive inline attributes. This is not only a more elegant way of handling static styles, but it can save us quite a few kilobytes along the way. In this particular sketch, taking this measure resulted in a 40% reduction in the rendered markup – not bad!

# Spinning Noise

In our next sketch, to consolidate some of the concepts covered already, we're going to spin some `line` elements about their center points and vary their line lengths and colors with noise. This time we'll use just a single loop and noise dimension.

Copy the previous sketch folder and name it something like
13-spinning-noise. Remove the style element and everything after the
background so that we're left with the following boilerplate code:

```
import { SvJs, Gen, Noise } from '../../node_modules/svjs/src/
index.js';

// Parent SVG.
const svg = new SvJs().addTo(document.
getElementById('container'));

// Viewport and viewBox (1:1 aspect ratio).
const svgSize = Math.min(window.innerWidth, window.innerHeight);
svg.set({ width: svgSize, height: svgSize, viewBox: '0 0 1000
1000' });

// Background.
svg.create('rect').set({
  x: 0, y: 0, width: 1000, height: 1000, fill: '#181818'
});
```

We'll then set up our noise-related variables, along with a couple of
randomized values that will determine our initial hue and the amount of
times our loop will run.

```
// Noise-related and randomised variables.
let noise = new Noise();
let nX = 0;
let noiseSpeed = 0.025;
let lines = svg.create('g');
let hue = Gen.random(0, 360);
let iterations = Gen.random(60, 100);
```

# Mapping and Constraining

We can now run the loop. We'll offset our iteration start point by 10 ; for this particular sketch, this value just worked better than starting at the usual 0. Within the loop, we'll fetch the noiseValue, and then we'll extract two further variables from this by individually mapping the value to different ranges. One will control how much we shift the hue, and the other will control the length of each line.

```
// Start the dance.
for (let i = 10; i < iterations; i += 1) {
  let noiseValue = noise.get(nX);
  let hueShift = Gen.map(noiseValue, -1, 1, -180, 180, false);
  let lineLength = Gen.map(noiseValue, -1, 1, 0, 1000, false);
}
```

After the lineLength variable (and still within the loop), set up the first of our lines. We will start off with a straight vertical line at (0, 0) (the top left of our viewBox), and we'll worry about centering things later. As it's a vertical line, the second x coordinate won't change – only the second y coordinate will.

Next comes the stroke value. We'll wrap this in the Gen.constrain() function to keep the values between 0 and 360, and inside this, the hue will increment by the hueShift. We'll then set both the opacity (within the hsl() function) and the stroke-width to 0.5, which will keep the line nice and delicate.

```
let l1 = lines.create('line').set({
  x1: 0, y1: 0, x2: 0, y2: lineLength,
  stroke: `hsl(${Gen.constrain(hue + hueShift, 0, 360)} 80% 80%
  / 0.5)`,
  stroke_width: 0.5
});
```

For the second line, we'll do much the same, except this time we'll stretch the lineLength a little, shift the hue in the opposite direction, and also reduce its opacity.

```
let l2 = lines.create('line').set({
  x1: 0, y1: 0, x2: 0, y2: lineLength * 1.1,
  stroke: `hsl(${Gen.constrain(hue - hueShift, 0, 360)} 80% 80%
  / 0.25)`,
  stroke_width: 0.5
});
```

# Rotating and Translating

The final step will involve some transforms and the usual incrementation of our noise coordinate. We'll rotate the first line positively in a clockwise direction and the second line negatively in an anticlockwise direction. For this, we'll use the SvJs rotate() method, which is simpler than setting a transform: rotate() attribute as we've done in some previous sketches. It also boasts some additional benefits:

- It rotates relative to its own center by default, rather than the top left of the canvas.

- It preserves any existing transforms, rather than overwriting them as the transform attribute does.

With that in mind, let's continue with the sketch and complete the loop.

```
l1.rotate(i);
l2.rotate(-i);

nX += noiseSpeed;
```

And finally, outside the loop, move the lines to the center of the canvas and rotate them by a random amount between 0 and 360.

```
lines.moveTo(500, 500);
lines.rotate(Gen.random(0, 360));
```

As you can see in Figure 5-4, what we end up are a series of slightly asymmetric lines that somewhat resemble, to me at least, the dance of some deep-sea creatures.

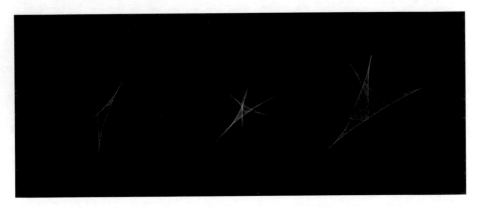

***Figure 5-4.***  *Spinning lines or deep-sea creatures?*

## Summary

While there's certainly more to explore where noise is concerned, we've covered the basics here, and we will be utilizing noise again in the forthcoming chapters. If you want to be able to tinker more with the nuts and bolts of noise, I'd encourage you to check out some third-party libraries like the popular SimplexJS, which goes beyond two dimensions and allows for greater freedom of configuration (at a cost of size, however).

Before we move on, let's quickly recap what we've covered in this chapter:

- The limits of randomness when creating more organic forms and how noise addresses this limitation

- The theory behind the abstract noise space

- How to put this into practice with the SvJs `Noise` module

- How to traverse the noise space within a loop

- How to use noise values to modify element coordinates and colors

- Mapping and constraining noise values to more useful ranges

- Optimizing repetitive element attributes with CSS

- Nondestructive element rotations

In the next chapter, we're going to cover a fundamental part of the SVG spec: the very powerful path element.

# CHAPTER 6

# The All-Powerful Path

Paths are perhaps the most important and most powerful part of the SVG spec. Most SVG files, be they simple icons or complex artworks, consist primarily of path data. If, for example, you draw anything more advanced than a primitive shape in a vector graphics program like Inkscape or Illustrator, you are ipso facto working with paths. And no, to program paths manually in JavaScript and SvJs, you don't need to be a mathematical wizard.

This chapter will cover the path element and its associated commands, which are sufficiently numerous to need their own subsections. Paths can get complicated quickly, so we'll also be covering some SvJs methods to make our lives easier.

## The Path Element

It's simple to set up a path; we just call the SvJs `create()` method as we would with most other elements:

```
let path = svg.create('path');
```

Paths accept the usual `fill` and `stroke` attributes that other graphical elements do, but unlike other graphical elements (like `rect` and `circle`), they come with no intrinsic form or shape. This is entirely up to us to define, and we do so via the `d` attribute.

© David Matthew 2024
D. Matthew, *Generative Art with JavaScript and SVG*, Design Thinking,
https://doi.org/10.1007/979-8-8688-0086-3_6

# D for Data

The d attribute allows us to populate a path with data. This data consists of a series of path commands and accompanying numeric values that define the form the path takes. The data as a whole is passed in as a string.

The creators of the SVG spec knew that paths would feature heavily in most SVG files, so creating concise path commands was a crucial part of keeping down the overall kilobyte count. They are therefore of single-character length, like the d attribute to which they are passed, and the values that accompany the commands can also be flexibly formatted to conserve space.

```
// An example of a string of path data.
path.set({
  d: 'M 20,20 L 30,20 L 30,30 L 20,30 Z'
});

// An identical path using a more concise string.
path.set({
  d: 'M20 20L30 20L30 30L20 30Z'
});
```

We'll go into more detail in later sections as to how examples like the aforementioned work; for now, just note that the very same path data can be written with or without commas to separate values and with or without spaces to separate commands.

# Path Commands

You can think of path commands as drawing instructions. Each command is represented by a letter, and this letter can be either uppercase or lowercase. The uppercase version indicates that the values which follow will use absolute coordinates (so the command M 50,50 would mean

138

moving to the exact position of 50,50 in the viewBox), whereas the lowercase version means that relative coordinates will be used (so the command m 50,50 would mean moving by +50 on both the x and y axes relative to the last known position).

There are a total of ten commands; twenty if you count the two versions. And if you think that sounds like a lot, you'd be right! It is a lot. But there's an amazing economy to these commands when you consider that they can be combined to create any possible two-dimensional shape. Some commands are more common than others, some more complex, and some we'll demonstrate the once and won't use again.

## Starting and Ending a Path

All paths start somewhere. And where SVG is concerned, all paths start at the point to which we move our virtual pen. We use the M (or m) command for this, which means "move to." We follow this with an x and y coordinate pair to define the path's starting point. The M command by itself doesn't draw anything – it merely moves us to the point at which we want to begin. Our pen has yet to push down on the paper, so to speak.

```
// Syntax for the M/m command.
'M [x, y] ...'
'm [dx, dy] ...'

// Examples of the M/m command.
'M 50 100 ...'
'm 50 100 ...'
```

We can provide an optional Z command at the very end of a path to close it. Paths without a closing Z command remain open (i.e., the starting point and end point remain unconnected). Z will draw a straight line to connect these two points unless the end point is a curve, in which case it will follow the curvature of the last control point (this will make more sense later on).

```
// Closing a path.
'M 50 100 ... 50 150 Z'
```

Unlike other path commands, the lowercase z and uppercase Z perform identical operations, as no values follow them. This means you can use them interchangeably.

# Straight Lines

To ease us into path creation, we'll start with the straight line. There are actually a few different commands that can draw a straight line, but we'll start with the most obvious.

# The Simple L

The L command allows us to draw straight lines defined by an x and y coordinate pair. The lowercase l does the same but uses coordinates relative to the path's last entered point.

```
// Syntax for the L/l command.
'L [x, y] ...'
'l [dx, dy] ...'
```

Let's see what this looks like in practice. In the following example, two lines are used to create two instances of the letter L. The first uses absolute coordinates; the second uses relative coordinates.

```
// The first L.
svg.create('path').set({
  d: 'M 300 200 L 300 800 L 600 800'
});

// The second L.
svg.create('path').set({
  d: 'M 675 825 l 0 -600 l -300 0'
});
```

We can see a rendering of the preceding code in Figure 6-1. I've left out any elements and attributes extraneous to the example and focused on just the path data. As you can see, you can use either of the L commands to achieve similar results.

When creating paths manually in this manner, some readers may find absolute coordinates more intuitive to work with, while others may find relative coordinates easier to use. Relative coordinates can be especially useful if, say, you wanted to move a path's location without disturbing its shape; with absolute coordinates, we'd have to change all the subsequent numbers, whereas with relative coordinates, we'd only have to change the initial M point.

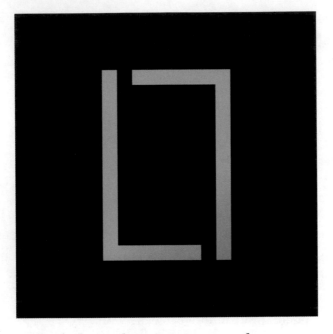

***Figure 6-1.*** *Two L's drawn by two L commands*

## Horizontal and Vertical Varieties

If the lines that we're drawing are either horizontal or vertical, we can use
the H or V commands as a shortcut, as they only need the one parameter;
in the case of H or h, the x coordinate, and in the case of V or v, the y
coordinate.

```
// Syntax for the H/h command.
'H [x] ...'
'h [dx] ...'

// Syntax for the V/v command.
'V [y] ...'
'v [dy] ...'
```

These commands I don't find particularly useful for generative art, but it's worth knowing they're there should you want to use them. Let's create the same L shapes from Figure 6-1, but with H and V this time, including their lowercase versions.

```
// The first L.
svg.create('path').set({
  d: 'M 300 200 V 800 H 600'
});
```

```
// The second L.
svg.create('path').set({
  d: 'M 675 825 v -600 h -300'
});
```

## Further Economies

Before we move on to curves, it's worth pointing out if we are using successive path commands of the same type, the command itself can be removed rather than repeated. SVG renderers are intelligent enough to know that if a path command is omitted, the last-known command should be used. Let's show a quick example (the output of which is shown in Figure 6-2).

```
// The first path, with repeating L commands.
svg.create('path').set({
  d: 'M 10 10 L 20 20 L 30 10 L 40 20 L 50 10 L 60 20 L 70 10'
});
```

```
// The second (identical) path, with the repeating L commands
omitted.
svg.create('path').set({
  d: 'M 10 10 L 20 20 30 10 40 20 50 10 60 20 70 10'
});
```

*Figure 6-2.*  *Omitting repetitive commands*

# Quadratic Bezier Curves

The first curve we'll cover is the quadratic Bezier curve. Don't worry – the rather daunting name doesn't reflect its complexity. As far as curves go, it's relatively simple. Two sets of coordinates are required: the first set defines the control point (which we'll explain in a moment), and the second the destination point.

```
// Syntax for the Q/q command.
'Q [cpx cpy x y] ...'
'q [dcpx dcpy dx dy] ...'
```

## Control Points

If you imagine a control point as a force of attraction, or pull, toward which a curve bends, you'll have the right idea. Control points aren't themselves rendered, but if you look at the dot and dashed line in Figure 6-3, you can see a visualization of the force a control point exerts over its curve (in this case, a quadratic Bezier curve). In this example, the dot represents the control point coordinates of [150, 350], given the following path:

```
'M 50 150 Q 150 350 250 150'
```

***Figure 6-3.*** *The control point of a quadratic Bezier curve*

A quadratic Bezier curve has just the one control point, whereas the cubic Bezier curve (explored in a later section), has two.

## A Smooth Shortcut

Say we wanted to extend the path from Figure 6-3 and draw a smooth set of waves repeating at regular intervals. The difficulty in doing this manually is with the calculation of the control point; if it's not perfectly symmetric with the previous one, a "kink" will appear in our curve (see Figure 6-4). Now, in this particular case, it's not that arduous a job to calculate a control point that would correct this, but in more complex cases, this can become a challenge.

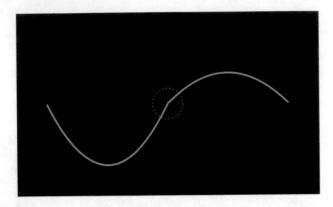

***Figure 6-4.*** *A kink in the curve*

This is where the T command can help us. It extends a quadratic Bezier curve based on the previous curve's control point, essentially "mirroring" or reflecting it. The result is a smooth curve with a symmetric control point, and it requires just a single set of coordinates.

```
// Syntax for the T/t command.
'T [x y]'
't [dx dy]'
```

Let's extend the curve from Figure 6-4, adding a few extra undulations to it. In the following example code, I'm adding some commas to the coordinates for the sake of readability, but remember that they're not actually required. I'm also taking advantage of the fact that I don't need to repeat the T command when using it several times consecutively. This is why you'll only see it used once for the four coordinates that follow.

```
// Extending a quadratic curve with the smooth T command.
svg.create('path').set({
    d: 'M 50,150 Q 150,350 250,150 T 450,150 650,150 850,150
    1050,150'
});
```

Figure 6-5 is the result, with some circular highlights added in to distinguish the initial M point (yellow) and the full Q curve (the purple second point) from the four additional T points (in red).

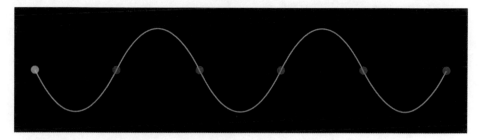

***Figure 6-5.***  *A smooth quadratic curve*

## A Quadratic Slinky

Let's use the quadratic Bezier curve in a simple sketch to create a Slinky-esque array of paths. If you don't know what a Slinky is, it's a popular spring-based toy that can "walk" itself down a set of steps if given a nudge from the top (I'm sure it can perform many other miraculous feats, but this is the one for which it's most widely known).

Copy the template folder and rename it to 14-quadratic-slinky. Below the parent SVG, set some styles to target the path elements that we'll later set up as children of a group to which we'll give an id of slinky.

```
// Style the slinky.
svg.create('style').content(`
  #slinky path {
    fill: none;
    stroke-width: 0.75;
    stroke-linecap: round;
  }`
);
```

Next set up the usual background, initialize a random hue, and create the aforementioned `slinky` group.

```
// Background.
svg.create('rect').set({
  x: 0, y: 0, width: 1000, height: 1000, fill: '#181818'
});

// Choose a random starting hue.
let hue = Gen.random(0, 360);

// Set up the slinky path group.
let slinky = svg.create('g').set({ id: 'slinky' });
```

In the next step, we'll fire up the loop and create a couple of control points we'll use to shape our quadratic curve.

```
// Start the loop.
for (let i = 0; i < 500; i += 5) {

  // Create the control points.
  let cpx = Gen.random(200, 400);
  let cpy = i - 400;

}
```

The width of our curve will be 600 units (relative to the `viewBox`), so our halfway point will be 300. On the x axis, the `cpx` variable is picking a random integer value 100 units either side of the halfway point, to give our slinky some "wobble." The `cpy` variable is more straightforward; it moves down the screen on each iteration, with an offset of 400 units that will "pull" the curve upward.

Next, let's create the actual curve (keeping within the loop).

```
// Create the quadratic curve.
slinky.create('path').set({
  stroke: `hsl(${hue} 90% 80% / 0.85)`,
  d: `M 0 ${i} q ${cpx} ${cpy} 600 0`
});
```

Here, we're setting the hue as we've done many times before, and for the path, we're drawing one simple curve starting with the M command. For the curve coordinates, we're taking advantage of the relative coordinates calculated by the lowercase q command, which allows us to keep the values in step with curve's starting point.

Before closing out the loop, we'll increment the hue, but we'll use a new technique to do so. I mentioned the modulo operator (%) in Chapter 2 (in the section covering operators), which calculates a number's remainder after division. This can be useful to cycle within predefined ranges, such as the 0 to 360 constraints of a color's hue. Add the following as the final line before the end of the loop:

```
// Increment the hue.
hue = (hue % 360) + 1.5;
```

A quick explanation of how this works: say our random hue is initialized to 350. The expression hue % 360 will return 350, because 350 / 360 is 0, with a remainder of 350. This works similarly for every number in our range *except* 360, which returns 1 when divided by itself and returns a remainder of 0. This is how it cycles back to the start of the range.

Now that our loop is done, we can add one more line outside it to ensure the content is centered. The result should resemble Figure 6-6.

```
slinky.moveTo(500, 500);
```

***Figure 6-6.*** *Quadratic curves in a slinky formation*

# Elliptical Arcs

Time to embark on the arc! The elliptical arc curve (Figure 6-7) is a
complicated beast, and the syntax is quite difficult to comprehend without
some visual examples. The A (or a) command is used to initialize it, and it
is followed by no less than seven arguments.

```
// Syntax for the A/a command.
'A [rx ry rotation large-arc-flag sweep-flag x y] ...'
'a [rx ry rotation large-arc-flag sweep-flag dx dy] ...'
```

The first two arguments and the last two arguments aren't anything we
haven't encountered before: rx and ry refer to the radii of the x and y axes,
and the final x and y arguments define the curve's destination point.

The rotation defines the angle of rotation along the x axis, and the large-arc-flag and sweep-flag are both booleans in numeric form, 0 meaning false and 1 meaning true. What they do though takes a little explaining.

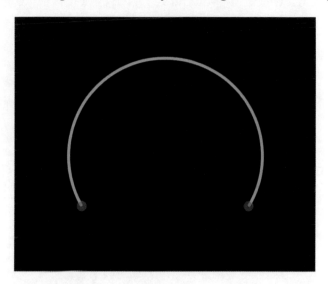

***Figure 6-7.*** *An elliptical arc curve*

## Setting the Flags

What's really happening when we draw an elliptical arc curve is that two interlocking ellipses are used as guides behind the scenes to determine which of the many possible paths are actually drawn. With the large-arc-flag set to 1, a large arc will be chosen. And with the sweep-flag set to 1, the arc will be drawn in a clockwise direction. Let's take a look at Figure 6-8, in which four possible permutations of these flags are shown.

- In the uppermost path, the large-arc-flag and sweep-flag are both set to 1.

- In the second path down, the large-arc-flag is set to 0 and the sweep-flag is set to 1.

151

- In the third path down, the `large-arc-flag` and the `sweep-flag` are both set to 0.

- In the lowermost path, the `large-arc-flag` is set to 1 and the `sweep-flag` is set to 0.

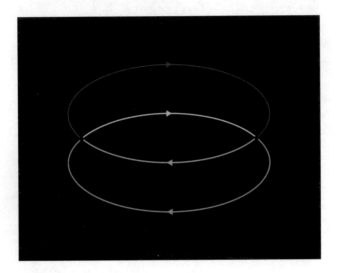

***Figure 6-8.***  *Four possible arcs*

In practice, you'll only ever see one of these arcs rendered on screen. However, it helps us understand the underlying structure of the elliptical arc when we see all the possible curves rendered simultaneously.

## Irregular Radii

One of the other potential confusions about the elliptical arc curve is that the two radius values `rx` and `ry` work a little differently to how we might expect. Normally, a radius would directly determine the size of an elliptical shape. In the case of the elliptical arc curve, the size is actually determined by a number of factors that work in conjunction, and the `rx` and `ry` values are only one part of the equation.

You'll sometimes find, for instance, that the interlocking ellipses that form the basis of the possible curves coincide; that is, they are superimposed on one another. You'll know this is the case if setting the large-arc-flag to either a 0 or a 1 makes no difference to the final result. This can happen when the two radius values and the distance between the curve start and end points are in a certain proportion to each other.

It might therefore be easier to think of the rx and ry values as ratios that influence the shape of the arc than as values that directly determine the arc's magnitude (this is especially true when using smaller radii values). Don't worry if this doesn't make much sense – it's quite counterintuitive at first and only becomes clearer with experimentation. And to aid in this experimentation and hopefully make the elliptical arc curve a little more accessible, I've created an interactive pen that shows the effect of altering both the radii and the flag values. You can find the pen at davidmatthew.ie/generative-art-javascript-svg#arc-curve.

## Generative Arcs

Let's take a break from further wrestling with the theoretical intricacies of elliptical arc curves and put them to some practical, creative use instead. Using our usual copy method, create a new sketch folder and name it something like 15-generative-arcs. The aim of this sketch will be to create two sets of arc curves: one set running clockwise and the other set mirroring it, running anticlockwise. We'll randomize a number of key variables to keep the output unique and difficult to predict.

When you're ready, set up a group below the background that will contain our arc curves. After that, we'll set up some randomized variables we'll utilize in the loop that follows.

```
// Set up a container group for our arc curves.
let arcs = svg.create('g');
```

```
// Randomise some variables.
let rx = Gen.random(5, 350);
let ry = Gen.random(5, 350);
let hue = Gen.random(0, 360);
```

Next we'll start our loop, which will run 360 times. Inside it, we'll randomize some further variables: the arc's `rotation`, which will have the effect of distending the curve in a particular direction, and the `large-arc-flag`, which, thanks to our `Gen.chance()` function, will have a 50% chance of being either 0 or 1.

```
for (let i = 0; i < 360; i += 1) {

  // Randomise the rotation and large arc flag.
  let rotation = Gen.random(0, 180);
  let largeArc = Gen.chance() ? 1 : 0;

}
```

Next (and still within our loop) create the first set of clockwise arc curves. Remember, what makes them run either clockwise or anticlockwise is the `sweep-flag`, which is the fifth argument of the A command. Here, after our `largeArc` variable, we're setting the `sweep-flag` to 1, meaning clockwise.

```
// Create a first set of clockwise arc curves (sweep = 1).
arcs.create('path').set({
  fill: 'none',
  stroke: `hsl(${hue} 75% 75% / 0.05)`,
  d: `M 275 500 A ${rx} ${ry} ${rotation} ${largeArc} 1
  725 500`
});
```

The second set of arc curves will be identical, bar two small changes. The sweep-flag we'll set to 0, making this set anticlockwise, and the hue we'll offset by 60, just to add a bit of contrast to the colors. And before we close out the loop, we'll increment the hue using the aforementioned modulo operator.

```
// Create a second set of counter-clockwise arc curves (sweep = 0).
arcs.create('path').set({
  fill: 'none',
  stroke: `hsl(${hue + 60} 75% 75% / 0.05)`,
  d: `M 275 500 A ${rx} ${ry} ${rotation} ${largeArc} 0 725 500`
});

// Increment the hue.
hue = (hue % 360) + 0.5;
```

If you run the sketch at this point, you'll see some nicely varied generative arcs (example output in Figure 6-9). If you want to inject a little more dynamism though, you could add the following line after the loop:

```
// Apply a random rotation.
arcs.rotate(Gen.random(0, 360));
```

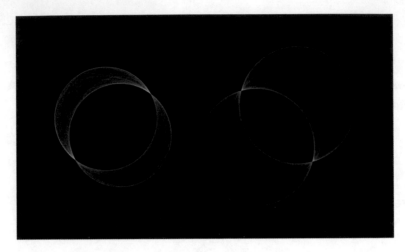

**Figure 6-9.**  *Two renders of our generative arcs*

# Cubic Bezier Curves

The final curve we'll cover is the cubic Bezier curve, called by the C command. This is the most versatile of all the vector curves available to us and is the main curve utilized in most vector drawing and illustration packages (usually under the alias of the pen tool). It has two sets of control points, so the syntax is a little more complex than its quadratic counterpart, but it's easier to grapple with than the elliptical arc curve.

```
// Syntax of the C/c command.
'C [cpx1 cpy1 cpx2 cpy2 x y] ...'
'c [dcpx1 dcpy1 dcpx2 dcpy2 dx dy] ...'
```

## Cubic Control Points

The first set of control point coordinates cpx1 and cpy1 shapes the curve from the side of the starting point. This starting point is declared prior to the C command – it might be a set of M coordinates, for example, or the end point of a previous curve. The second set of control point coordinates cpx2 and cpy2 shapes the curve of the destination point, and this point is defined by the final two coordinates: x and y. Here's an example:

```
// Creating a single cubic bezier curve.
svg.create('path').set({
  d: 'M 75,75 C 140,330 360,330 425,75'
});
```

The preceding path is illustrated in Figure 6-10, where you can see the initial M point in yellow, and in red, the three points that comprise the cubic Bezier curve itself. The colored dots and dashed lines are just for illustrative purposes; these wouldn't be rendered in the final SVG.

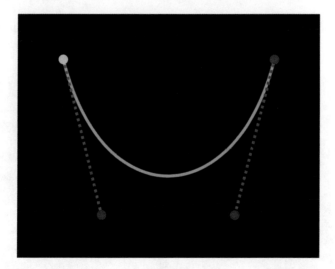

***Figure 6-10.*** *A cubic Bezier curve with the control points visualized*

When linked together, consecutive cubic Bezier curves can combine to create any 2D shape imaginable. They are such a staple of vector drawing programs that wielding them effectively has become a craft in itself. Judicious use of these curves and their "handles" (visualized as the dashed lines in Figure 6-10) can make the difference between smooth, graceful line art and awkward, clunky clip art.

157

# S for Symmetry

Like the quadratic Bezier curve, the cubic Bezier curve has a related command that can be called if you want to extend the curve with another that is smoothly connected to it. The command to use for this is S (or s for relative values). The S command automatically generates a symmetric control point that mirrors the control point of the preceding curve and as a result allows us to omit the first set of control point coordinates.

```
// Extending a cubic bezier curve with the S command.
svg.create('path').set({
  d: 'M 50,150 C 100,250 200,50 250,150 S 400,50 450,150'
});
```

In Figure 6-11, the faintest of the dashed lines indicates where the S command has automatically generated a symmetrical control point.

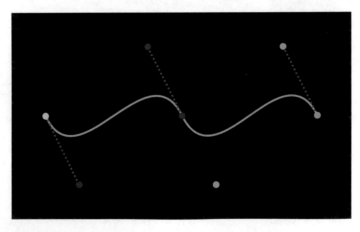

***Figure 6-11.*** *A smoothly extended cubic Bezier curve*

# Organic Curves

Let's put the preceding knowledge to use in a composition, the aim of which will be to create a series of smooth, organic-looking curves. To this end, our friend Noise will nudge us in the right direction. First, do the usual and copy the template folder, calling it something like 16-organic-curves. Ensure you have the following imports at the top:

```
import { SvJs, Gen, Noise } from '../../node_modules/svjs/src/
index.js';
```

The parent SVG and background will then follow, at which point we'll create some noise-related variables. I'm including a new one here called amplifier; this will be used when we map the noise value to a new range (increasing its volume so to speak).

```
// Noise-related.
let noise = new Noise();
let n = Gen.random(0, 1000);
let speed = 0.05;
let amplifier = Gen.random(200, 500);
```

Next we'll set up variables relating to colors and the curves themselves, which we'll contain within a group.

```
// Curve and colour-related.
let curves = svg.create('g');
let numCurves = Gen.random(75, 125);
let hue = Gen.random(0, 360);
```

It's generally good practice to group your variables meaningfully in this manner, with some comments to add clarity. Otherwise when you later revisit your code, you might have a hard time working out your original intentions. You could go a step further and group them via objects (a technique outlined in Chapter 2), but I won't do that here.

We'll move on to the loop next, where we'll first retrieve and then re-map our noise into a more fit-for-purpose range (using the aforementioned `amplifier` variable). Notice here that the range will span positive and negative values, so we won't know the polarity in advance. In the case of our curves, this will help us mimic a more organic movement, as the values won't always be uniformly offset from the original starting point, but wrap around them more naturally. Outside the loop, include the `moveTo()` method to center-align our curve group.

```
for (let i = 0; i < numCurves; i += 1) {

  // Retrieve and map our noise value.
  let noiseValue = noise.get(n);
  noiseValue = Gen.map(noiseValue, -1, 1, -amplifier,
  amplifier, false);

}

curves.moveTo(500, 500);
```

Next come the curve coordinates. For clarity, we'll set variables for each command we call, to make the construction of the path data (or d string) less unwieldy. Continue with the following code, keeping it within the loop. The shape of the curve we're aiming for isn't too dissimilar to the one shown in Figure 6-10. Other than that, the values provided are fairly arbitrary, so feel free to tweak them.

```
// M command co-ordinates.
let mx = 0;
let my = 0 + (i * 5);

// C command co-ordinates.
let cpx1 = 0 + noiseValue;
let cpy1 = -100;
let cpx2 = 250 + noiseValue;
```

```
let cpy2 = -100;
let x2 = 300;
let y2 = 0;

// S command co-ordinates.
let spx = 350 + noiseValue;
let spy = 100;
let x3 = 300;
let y3 = -50;
```

With the exception of the initial M command coordinates, we're going to build out our curves using relative coordinates (i.e., we'll feed the preceding curve variables to the c and s commands rather than to their uppercase brethren). These tend to work better in a loop setting, as they always remain in step with the most recent coordinate values. The only other point to note is that we're being quite selective with which values are being modulated by our noiseValue variable, three out of a possible ten in this case. Sometimes subtlety works best, but again, feel free to experiment here.

With our variables in place, it's time to create the curve itself. I'll introduce a new technique here with regard to the use of template literal syntax. In previous sketches, we've been opening and closing our braces ${} for each variable. When these variables follow one after the other however, we can actually embed them all at once as an array.

```
// Create the organic curve.
curves.create('path').set({
  fill: 'none',
  stroke: `hsl(${hue} 80% 80% / 0.8)`,
  d: `M ${[mx, my]}
      c ${[cpx1, cpy1, cpx2, cpy2, x2, y2]}
      s ${[spx, spy, x3, y3]}`
});
```

If you run the sketch at this point, you'll see a series of curves alright, but their shape and color will remain uniform throughout. We haven't yet incremented our noise coordinate value – a vital step, but one all too easy to forget (I've omitted this line numerous times myself, leading to many a head-scratching moment). We'll take care of this step next and also increase the hue while we're at it, modulating it slightly via the noiseValue variable. As a final flourish, we'll throw in some randomized "bubbles" (see Figure 6-12). Don't ask me why.

```
// Increment the noise and hue.
n += speed;
hue = (hue % 360) + (noiseValue / 25);

// 10% chance of spawning a 'bubble'.
if (Gen.chance(10)) {
  svg.create('circle').set({
    r: Gen.random(5, 50),
    cx: Gen.random(150, 850),
    cy: Gen.random(150, 850),
    fill: `hsl(0 0% 100% / 0.1)`,
    stroke: '#888'
  });
}
```

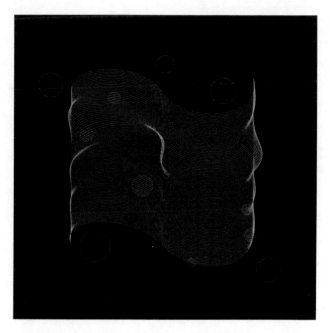

**Figure 6-12.** *Noise-modulated organic curves*

# An Easier Option

Having to juggle six coordinates for every curve segment (or four when we use the S command) can get a little trying at times. Wouldn't it be nice to be able to connect a series of single points with a smooth curve, without having to worry about all those extra control points?

Glad you asked! SvJs comes equipped with a method called createCurve() that can do just this. Under the hood, it harnesses the power of the cubic Bezier curve but abstracts away the control points so that constructing a curve is a less intimidating affair. This does sacrifice a large degree of control, but in some cases, we may not need the level of fine-tuning that the manual curve commands offer. With the createCurve() method, all we need to worry about are the points.

```
// The syntax of the createCurve() method.
createCurve(pointsArray, [curveFactor]);
```

In crude terms, we can think of this as a join-the-dots method, the main difference being that we need to supply the dots rather than do the joining. The first argument, pointsArray, is, as the name suggests, an array of [x, y] coordinate pairs. It can be supplied as either a standard one-dimensional array or as a two-dimensional array (i.e., an array of arrays).

```
// A one-dimensional array of points.
let points1D = [25, 30, 45, 20, 80, 10, 90, 40];
```

```
// A two-dimensional array of the same points.
let points2D = [
  [25, 30], [45, 20], [80, 10], [90, 40]
];
```

The curveFactor argument allows us to modify the tension between the points. At a value of 0, the points are connected by a straight line. At a value of 1 (the default), the tension is looser and the curve much smoother. In general, the most usable results lie in the range of 0 to 2; stray too far beyond that and the underlying control points will overlap and create some truly chaotic squiggles. On certain occasions though, this may be what you want.

In Figure 6-13, we can see the aforementioned curveFactor values in action. The uppermost curve is set to 0, the middle curve to 1, and the bottom curve to 5. The faint dots indicate where our pointsArray coordinates are positioned and are shown for illustrative purposes only; you wouldn't see these rendered normally.

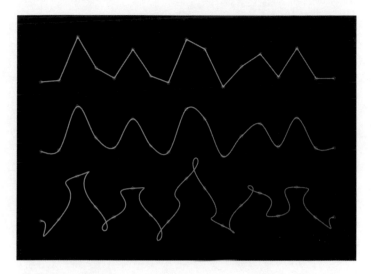

*Figure 6-13. Varying the curve factor using values of 0, 1, and 5*

# Summary

With paths now a part of your generative arsenal, so many more possibilities open up for you. To recap, we've covered the following:

- The path data (d) string format and the flexibility and economies it offers.

- The difference between absolute and relative path commands

- The L, V, and H straight-line commands

- The Q and T quadratic Bezier curve commands.

- What control points are and how to harness them

- The elliptical arc curve command A and its complex array of arguments

- The C and S cubic Bezier curve commands

- Using noise and randomness to shape curves

- The SvJs `createCurve()` method

In the next chapter, we'll explore motion, animation, and how to make our sketches interactive.

# CHAPTER 7

# Motion and Interactivity

One characteristic that tends to distinguish generative art from other art forms is its ability to incorporate interactivity, and, as a result, active audience participation. This audience – whether it be a single user on a laptop or a small crowd at an art installation – can then influence, or even determine, the end result. In essence, such art is *dynamic*; it moves; it responds; it flows. It isn't fixed and final.

In this chapter, we'll explore some of the underlying techniques of interactive art, including event listeners, callback functions, cursor tracking, collision detection, and how to use these to alter our SVG elements and attributes in real time. We'll also delve into the different methods that can be used to animate SVG and discuss their strengths and weaknesses before deciding on the method we'll adopt for the remainder of the chapter.

## Event Listeners

A mouse click is an event, as is hitting a key on your keyboard, or tapping your tablet's touchscreen display. When events like this occur in the context of a web browser, as JavaScript programmers, we can prick up our virtual ears and listen out for them. And as soon as an event is detected, we can capture it. What we do once we've captured an event is up to us.

© David Matthew 2024
D. Matthew, *Generative Art with JavaScript and SVG*, Design Thinking,
https://doi.org/10.1007/979-8-8688-0086-3_7

We could use it to trigger any number of things – a custom message, a color change, a simple animation, a complex transformation; the possibilities are endless. But first we need to know how to "listen."

Thankfully this is straightforward: we can utilize a browser-native function called addEventListener(). This function needs three things: one, an element to attach itself to (i.e., the element that will do the listening); two, the event type to listen out for (e.g., a mouse click); and three, what to do when it hears it (i.e., the action performed by the callback function). It takes the following form:

```
// Adding an event listener to a HTML or SVG element.
element.addEventListener('eventType', doSomething);
```

We are assuming here that the callback function doSomething() is defined elsewhere in the code. Note that in this case it is supplied by name only, without the parentheses. This is so that the function doesn't trigger prematurely. The situation is different with anonymous – or arrow – functions, which can be defined there and then without the danger of being immediately invoked.

```
// Using arrow syntax to define the callback function.
element.addEventListener('eventType', () => {
  // do something here...
});
```

## Event Types

There are numerous types of events we can choose to listen out for, but we will focus on a small subset useful for generative art: keyboard, form, and pointer event types.

Keyboard event types like keydown and keyup capture the different phases of hitting a key as you type. Form event types like change and input can capture updates to interface elements for inputting data, such as sliders, text fields, and drop-downs. And pointer event types, perhaps the most significant of the lot where generative art is concerned, are a more modern alternative to mouse and touchscreen event types that aim to be more hardware-agnostic. Pointer event types include `pointerdown`, `pointermove`, `pointerover`, and `pointerup`, and for our purposes, we can also consider the `click` event type – technically a mouse event – as falling under this umbrella, as it can also capture simple touch events like a finger tap.

```
// Capturing the movement of a mouse, stylus or finger over an
element.
element.addEventListener('pointermove', () => {
  // do something here...
});
```

## Event Parameters

When an event listener is attached to an element and captures an event, that event can then be passed to the callback function as an argument. For example, if we were to add an event listener to our HTML `document.body` to detect `click` events, the properties of that `click` event would also be captured and could be put to use by the callback function.

Here's how this could work in practice. In the following code, the position of the mouse or pointer device is logged to the console each time you click anywhere within the body of the HTML page.

```
// Log the user's pointer co-ordinates on click.
document.body.addEventListener('click', (event) => {
  let x = event.clientX;
  let y = event.clientY;
  console.log(`x: ${x}, y: ${y}`);
});
```

169

The clientX and clientY properties are just a couple of the many properties built into a click event. The full list can be found over at MDN (developer.mozilla.org/docs/Web/API/Element/click_event), including comprehensive documentation covering the full range of DOM events.

# Triggering the SvJs Save Method

Say we have a sketch we're happy with, and we wanted to save the actual SVG markup generated by our JavaScript – how would we go about it? Perhaps the quickest way is to open up our browser's developer tools, select the Elements tab, and inspect the DOM tree until we locate the root SVG element. Then we can right-click it, select "Copy", and choose the nested "Copy outerHTML" option. This gives us the SVG file data that we want, but not the file itself, so as a final step, we need to open up a text or code editor, paste our clipboard contents into it, and *then* save it as an SVG file. Not exactly convenient.

It would be far easier to just hit a key on our keyboard and have the process happen automatically. SvJs does has a save() method that can be used for this purpose, but it first needs to be "wired up" to an event listener in order to fire. Let's do this now.

Open up any one of our previous sketches, and at the bottom of the sketch, let's write a function to call this method whenever we hit the "s" key. The event type will be keydown, which is triggered when any key is pressed, so we need to make sure we pass the event as an argument to our callback function so that we can query its key property; this is what tells us the actual key that was pressed. We'll trigger the save() method only when that key is equal to "s", irrespective of case (allowing us to capture the capital "S" too).

```
// Save the root svg as a downloadable file.
document.addEventListener('keydown', (event) => {
  let key = event.key.toLowerCase();
  if (key === 's') svg.save();
});
```

Feel free to use the aforementioned for any sketch going forward. And incidentally, the save() method can be called on any SVG element, meaning you can save just a portion of your SVG if you prefer – though the use cases for this are rarer.

# Creative Cursor Tracking

In our first example of an event listener in action, we showed how tracking the mouse cursor might be achieved. We simply had to query the clientX and clientY coordinates of the mouse event. This was purposely simplified, as accurately tracking the position of our mouse relative to the SVG viewport (which uses its own coordinate space) is a bit trickier.

## The SvJs trackCursor() Method

To solve this, SvJs has a built-in trackCursor() method that can be called on the root SVG element. It automatically takes care of attaching the relevant event listeners (pointermove and pointerleave), transforming the cursor position into the viewBox coordinate space, and ensuring the expected behavior also occurs with touchscreen devices. To activate it, it just needs to be called on the main SVG element as follows:

```
svg.trackCursor();
```

Once activated, it updates two properties of the parent SVG: cursorX and cursorY, which tell us where in the viewBox (rather than the web browser window) our cursor is currently located. It also allows us to pass in our own custom callback function, to be triggered each time the cursor position is updated.

```
// Passing in a custom callback.
svg.trackCursor(() => {
  // ... do stuff
});
```

# Interactive Ellipses

Let's set up a new sketch to show how trackCursor() can be put
to creative use. Copy our template folder and call it something like
17-cursor-tracking. We're going to re-create a variation of our very first
sketch from Chapter 1, but this time we'll make it interactive.

Below the background, initialize the following variables. The ellipses
array is a new addition; we'll use this to store the created ellipses so we can
iterate through them afterward.

```
// Randomise some variables.
let hue = Gen.random(0, 360);
let rotation = Gen.random(0, 360);
let iterations = Gen.random(50, 100);

// This array will allow us to iterate through our
ellipses later.
let ellipses = [];
```

Now for the loop to create the ellipses. The code here is more compact
than that presented in the first chapter, as we've since covered more
concise ways of achieving certain results (like incrementing our hue).
Another difference of note is the addition of the ellipses.push() method;
this is where we add each ellipse to the aforementioned array.

```
// Run a loop a random number of times to create the ellipses.
for (let i = 0; i < iterations; i += 1) {

  // Create our ellipse.
  let ellipse = svg.create('ellipse');
  ellipse.set({
    cx: 500,
    cy: 500,
    rx: 100 + (i * 3),
```

```
    ry: 300 + (i * 2),
    fill: 'none',
    stroke: `hsl(${hue} 80% 80% / 0.6)`,
    transform: `rotate(${rotation + (i * 2)} 500 500)`
  });

  // Add the ellipse to the array.
  ellipses.push(ellipse);

  // Increment the hue.
  hue = (hue % 360) + 2;
}
```

You should now see a static arrangement of ellipses. Our next step is make them dynamic. What we'll do is activate the `trackCursor()` method on the main SVG and pass in an arrow function as a callback. Inside this arrow function, we'll iterate through each item in the `ellipses` array using a `forEach()` loop and adjust the `cx` and `cy` coordinates of each ellipse relative to our cursor position.

```
// Adjust the centre point of each ellipse relative to
our cursor.
svg.trackCursor(() => {
  ellipses.forEach((ellipse) => {
    ellipse.set({
      cx: svg.cursorX,
      cy: svg.cursorY
    });
  });
});
```

And with this, we have movement – our ellipses glide gracefully into life as we create a truly dynamic cursor-guided composition! Figure 7-1 illustrates one possible variation with the cursor just south of center. A key-mapped save function is particularly useful here (I used it myself to save down Figure 7-1), as it allows us to capture our SVG without disturbing the composition with inadvertent cursor movement (as might happen if we had to click a button).

***Figure 7-1.*** *A cursor-transformed array of ellipses*

Now that we know how to achieve movement via interactivity, it's time to learn how to make things move independently of our input.

# Programming Motion

As mentioned previously, we have several different methods at our disposal for animating SVG. The first one we'll explore is CSS keyframes, which will be familiar territory to most web developers. The second is the method native to the SVG format itself – SMIL. The third is the Web Animations API (or WAAPI), which is a modern JavaScript-driven API. And the final method is a technique popular among generative artists (of the JavaScript variety at least): the recursive `requestAnimationFrame` method.

Knowledge of each technique and their respective strengths and weaknesses should serve you well, irrespective of which one we proceed with. We'll set up a simple sketch that will showcase, in a very rudimentary way, all four options. When you're ready, set up a new instance of our template sketch and call it something like `18-making-things-move`.

What we're going to do is create a diamond shape comprised of four overlaid squares of different dimensions (as shown in Figure 7-2) and animate each one using a different technique. The following code sets things up, and apart from the `transform_origin` attribute (which will ensure more consistent animation behavior across the various methods by setting a default point of rotation), there's nothing really new here, so feel free to simply copy and paste:

```
import { SvJs } from '../../node_modules/svjs/src/index.js';

// Parent SVG.
const svg = new SvJs().addTo(document.
getElementById('container'));

// Viewport and viewBox (1:1 aspect ratio).
const svgSize = Math.min(window.innerWidth, window.
innerHeight);
svg.set({ width: svgSize, height: svgSize, viewBox: '0 0 1000
1000' });

// Background.
svg.create('rect').set({
  x: 0, y: 0, width: 1000, height: 1000, fill: '#181818'
});
```

```
// Arrays to contain our shapes and their colours.
let palette = ['#34d399','#6ee7b7','#a7f3d0', '#d1fae5'];
let shapes = [];

// Initialise our four shapes.
for (let i = 0; i < 4; i += 1) {
  let size = 500 - (i * 125);
  let position = 250 + (i * 62.5);
  let shape = svg.create('rect').set({
    x: position,
    y: position,
    width: size,
    height: size,
    fill: palette[i],
    transform_origin: '50% 50%',
    transform: 'rotate(45)'
  });
  shapes.push(shape);
}
```

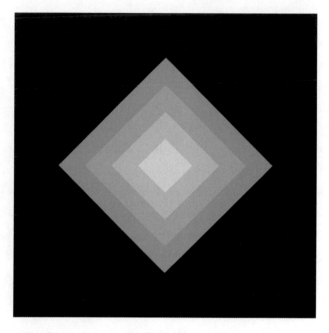

***Figure 7-2.***  *The four shapes we'll make move*

## CSS Keyframes

Animated sequences can be created with CSS using a @keyframes rule. Much like traditional keyframes used in animation, motion graphics, and video editing software, CSS @keyframes define the state of certain properties at a particular point in time (or step in a sequence). For example, at time t, our subject might be at position [x1, y1], and at time t + 5, the subject might have moved to [x2, y2]. Keyframes define these points in time, and the transition between one state and another is what constitutes the animation. We call this process "tweening" (meaning "inbetweening"), as the animation occurs in these inbetween states.

The syntax for CSS @keyframes is quite self-explanatory. You can set the start and end keyframes of a simple animation with from and to directives, or if you have something a little more complex in mind, you can use percentages to specify the point at which certain transitions should trigger. Once the @keyframes rule is defined, it then needs to be called by an element using the animation-name property, and we also need to specify how long the animation should take (the animation-duration). There are other optional properties that we can define, such as the animation-timing-function (also known as easing), which describes *how* we transition from one property value to another, and the animation-iteration-count, which specifies how many times our animation should play.

In the following code, we're calling the first shape of our array and assigning it an id of cssShape. This will enable us to easily target the element later. We then set up a @keyframes rule called scaleRotate that rotates its target a full 360 degrees, while simultaneously scaling it down along its x axis and up along its y axis (creating a stretching effect) before returning it to its original dimensions. And finally we assign the animation to the cssShape element, specifying the duration, iteration count, and timing function.

```
// Set an id for our first shape.
shapes[0].set({ id: 'cssShape' });

// Animate this shape with CSS.
svg.create('style').content(`
  @keyframes scaleRotate {
    0% { transform: rotate(0) scale(1, 1) }
    50% { transform: rotate(180deg) scale(0.5, 1.5) }
    100% { transform: rotate(360deg) scale(1, 1) }
  }

  #cssShape {
    animation-name: scaleRotate;
    animation-duration: 5s;
    animation-iteration-count: infinite;
        animation-timing-function: linear;
  }
`);
```

You should now see our outer square slowly rotate and stretch, while the others remain static. It's also possible to use the shorthand `animation` property, which allows for greater concision by declaring all our animation values at once. Only use this when familiar with the longhand version though, as the order of values – while not especially strict – can lead to unanticipated behavior if you're not familiar with all the possible values that can be accepted.

```
svg.create('style').content(`
  ...

  #cssShape {
    animation: scaleRotate 5s infinite linear;
  }
`);
```

## The SMIL Way

Now let's try to achieve the same thing with SMIL. SMIL, which stands for Synchronized Multimedia Integration Language, is the animation method native to SVG itself, requiring no CSS or JavaScript. However, as we're using SvJs, we will be interfacing with SMIL via JavaScript. Before we do so however, here's a quick peek at how it looks in its original form.

```
<circle cx="50" cy="50" r="25" fill="red">
  <animate
    attributeName="r"
    from="25"
    to="40"
    dur="2s"
    repeatCount="indefinite" />
</circle>
```

As you can see, the animation is an actual SVG element, nested inside the element it animates (a <circle> in this case). The <animate> element takes care of the animation of most SVG attributes, but in the case of element transforms (i.e., translating, rotating, scaling, or skewing), an <animateTransform> element must be used instead. There is one other animation element called <animateMotion>, reserved for animating an element along a path. As we will be rotating and scaling our shape, the <animateTransform> element is the one we'll be using.

Each transform requires its own element, making the syntax a little verbose. With the first transform, namely, the rotation, we specify the attributeName to animate and its type, rotate. We have just two states to transition between – 0 degrees and 360 degrees – so we can use from and to directives to cover these. We then set the duration (dur) and iteration count (repeatCount), and that's the first transform taken care of.

```
// Rotate the second shape using SMIL.
shapes[1].create('animateTransform').set({
  attributeName: 'transform',
  type: 'rotate',
  from: '0',
  to: '360',
  dur: '5s',
  repeatCount: 'indefinite'
});
```

The second transform is a little more complicated. It has more than two states, so instead of the from and to attributes, we have a values attribute that can store multiple states. In this case, we supply it with a semicolon-separated list of our transform values. We also need to include an additional additive attribute with a value of sum so that the scale transform adds to (and doesn't overwrite) the previous rotate transform.

```
// Scale the second shape using SMIL.
shapes[1].create('animateTransform').set({
  attributeName: 'transform',
  type: 'scale',
  values: '1 1; 0.5 1.5; 1 1',
  dur: '5s', additive: 'sum',
  repeatCount: 'indefinite'
});
```

The second shape should now be slowly rotating and stretching, and the motion should be perfectly synchronized with our CSS keyframes example.

## The Web Animations API

The Web Animations API, or WAAPI, is the most modern of the methods we'll be covering. It is being actively worked on by the W3C (World Wide Web Consortium) and is intended to provide the future direction for animation on the Web. In addition to keyframes and timing options, it supports advanced features such as control over playback rates, flexible easing functionality, scroll-linked timelines, and the ability to apply successive animations (or sequences) to the same element.

Elements can be animated with a sensibly named animate() method, which takes two arguments. The first argument defines the keyframes, and the second defines the timing options.

```
element.animate(keyframes, options);
```

The keyframes can be supplied as either an array of objects or an object containing arrays. And the timing options can be supplied as a single value – specifically, an integer defining the length of the animation in milliseconds – or as an object containing one or more time-related properties. Say we wanted to animate the value of a circle's radius r. The following is how this could be achieved using both syntax formats:

```
// Format one for keyframes.
let keyframes = [
  { r: 25 },
  { r: 40 },
  { r: 25 }
];

// Format two for keyframes.
let keyframes = {
  r: [25, 40, 25]
};

// Format one for timing options.
let options = 2000; // 2 seconds.

// Format two for timing options.
let options = {
  duration: 2000,
  iterations: Infinity,
  // ... etc
};
```

I prefer the second keyframe format as it is more concise in most cases. Before we implement the rotation and scaling example, there's one more thing to point out: how the keyframes are spaced out (or offset) from one another. With CSS keyframes, we need to explicitly state when a keyframe should trigger by using percentage values or the from and to directives. With the Web Animations API, the offset of animations is *inferred* if not explicitly stated. If we have three keyframes, they will be automatically spaced out at 0, 0.5, and 1, respectively (the equivalent of 0%, 50%, and 100% in CSS). But we can define custom offsets if needs be. In the following example, the second keyframe will trigger at 0.75 instead of the default 0.5.

```
// Explicitly defining offsets.
let keyframes = {
  r: [25, 40, 25],
  offset: [0, 0.75, 1]
};
```

Let's get back to our sketch now and implement the rotation and scaling of our third shape using the WAAPI method. Below our SMIL implementation, set up the animation as follows.

```
let keyframes = {
  transform: [
    'rotate(0deg) scale(1, 1)',
    'rotate(180deg) scale(0.5, 1.5)',
    'rotate(360deg) scale(1, 1)'
  ]
};

let options = {
  duration: 5000,
  iterations: Infinity
};

shapes[2].animate(keyframes, options);
```

Now all but one of our shapes should be on the move. Note how similar the WAAPI keyframes syntax is to our CSS keyframes example; this isn't by accident. The Web Animations API is essentially a further development of and extension to preexisting web animation standards so that web developers familiar with CSS animation should find the syntax intuitive and (mostly) compatible with what they already know. Having a native, high-level JavaScript API to create animations in the browser has opened up possibilities previously only attainable through the use of third-party libraries, but it isn't the only game in town where native JavaScript animation techniques are concerned.

# The requestAnimationFrame( ) Method

Meet the `requestAnimationFrame()` method, a low-level recursive technique that allows us to tap into the browser's screen repainting process. This is a very different approach from the methods we've covered previously; it is at the same time very simple and very complex. By calling a single method over and over again (this is the recursive part), we are handed full, fine-grained control over the entire animation process – but this also means we have to do everything ourselves. Concepts like keyframes and timing options don't really apply at this level.

The `requestAnimationFrame()` method must be called within a custom function we define, which contains the code we want to run on a per-frame basis. We then pass this custom function as an argument to `requestAnimationFrame`, so it is called recursively on each screen repaint. Here's a basic example of how this works.

```
// Define the function.
function customFunction() {

  // do stuff here...

  // Make the recursive call to requestAnimationFrame()).
  requestAnimationFrame(customFunction);
}

// Call the function.
customFunction();
```

Additionally, requestAnimationFrame() can pass a timestamp to our custom function so that we can sync our animation with real-time values rather than relying on the screen refresh rate, which can vary from device to device. The timestamp contains the amount of milliseconds that have elapsed since our animation started. Let's continue now with our sketch and set up an animate() function and pass it the timestamp so that we can use it to increment the angle of rotation. This works because rotation values can increment indefinitely beyond 360° and still remain valid.

```
// Animate the last shape using requestAnimationFrame.
function animate(time) {

  // Rotate the angle.
  let angle = time;

  // Apply the rotation.
  shapes[3].set({ transform: `rotate(${angle})` });

  // The recursive bit.
  requestAnimationFrame(animate);
}
animate();
```

Ok, so this code gets our final shape moving, but we've got a couple of problems. One, our shape is rotating at a breakneck speed, wildly out of sync with the others. And two, if you inspect the console, you'll see an error to the effect that we're supplying an undefined variable to our rotation transform. This error occurs just the once, so what that tells us is that when our function runs for the first time, the angle (and therefore the time) is undefined. This is simple enough to rectify; we just need to reassign the time variable to a value of 0 if it is undefined. Include the following code before the angle is declared, and that should soothe our console's concerns:

```
// Prevent errors when the time is undefined on first frame.
if (time === undefined) time = 0;
```

185

Now let's address the speed of rotation. We could try dividing the time by arbitrary amounts until it slows down to the point of synchronization (or something close enough), but that's not very satisfactory. Instead, let's work with what we know:

- Our shape should rotate by 360°.

- This rotation should take five seconds (or five thousand milliseconds).

- The time is provided in milliseconds.

Based on the aforementioned, we can derive a calculation that gives us the exact speed by which to rotate our shape: 0.072° per millisecond (360° divided by 5,000 milliseconds). Update the previous statement where angle simply equals time with the following:

```
// Rotate 360° in 5000ms: 360/5000 = 0.072.
let angle = time * 0.072;
```

This should rotate our shape in sync with the others. Getting it to scale in sync, however, is more of a challenge. For that, we first need to initialize some variables outside of the animation loop that can help us keep track of certain states. Why? Well, if we tried creating these states inside the loop, they would get overwritten on each iteration.

The scale increment value needs to swing back and forth between an upper and a lower limit, and the most straightforward way to achieve this is to keep track of the current scale value and its polarity (i.e., whether it's swinging one way or another). For this, we'll need a boolean that we can toggle back and forth like a switch. We'll also need a way to increment the scale value in a way that synchronizes with the time but doesn't use the timestamp value directly as this would only increment it indefinitely.

With the aforementioned in mind, let's initialize the following variables before the animate() function:

```
let isPositive = true;
let scale = 0, tick = 0, prevTime = 0;
```

Update the animation loop as follows. The comments do the explanatory heavy-lifting here, so to better understand each step, be sure to read the comments carefully. The main takeaway here is just how much more work we need to do with requestAnimationFrame() compared to the other methods.

```
// Animate the final shape using requestAnimationFrame.
function animate(time) {

  // Prevent errors when the time is undefined on first frame.
  if (time === undefined) time = 0;

  // Rotate 360° in 5000ms: 360/5000 = 0.072.
  let angle = time * 0.072;

  // We need a constant tick value that doesn't increment
     indefinitely.
  tick = time - prevTime;

  // Scale by 0.5 in 2500ms: 0.5/2500 = 0.0002.
  scale = isPositive ? scale + (tick * 0.0002) : scale -
  (tick * 0.0002);

  // Apply the rotation and scale values.
  shapes[3].set({
    transform: `rotate(${angle}) scale(${1 - scale},
    ${1 + scale})`
  });
```

```
// Flip the polarity if the scale value falls outside
   these bounds.
if (scale < 0 || scale > 0.5) isPositive = !isPositive;
// Capture the time before it increments.
prevTime = time;

// The recursive bit.
requestAnimationFrame(animate);
}
```

```
animate();
```

We should now have the final shape rotating and scaling in sync (give or take) with the other shapes. In some cases, you might see some slight offset in the rotation, or the scaling might happen a little quicker than expected. Discrepancies like this have more to do with how the browser automatically schedules and handles optimizations with the other animation methods than it has to do with the performance of requestAnimationFrame() itself. These animation methods weren't designed to be combined as we've done in this sketch; normally you'll choose one method and stick to it, depending on what you're trying to achieve.

## Methods Summarized

So which method should you choose for generative art? There's no definitive answer to this, but for what it's worth, here's my advice (with the caveat that this is not a comprehensive analysis of the pros and cons of each method, but a cursory comparison from my inevitably partisan point of view).

CSS keyframes are more suited to shorter sequences, such as animated loading indicators (an art in themselves), UX enhancements, and animations where accessibility or browser compatibility is a concern. For more elaborate sequences, they can quickly get convoluted and awkward to edit. For animating SVG specifically, there are many attributes that are inaccessible when using CSS, such as masks, clip paths, and gradients.

With SMIL, you've got a well-thought-out animation format native to SVG and one that can access all animation-capable attributes. Unlike the other methods, it can also retain its animations when the SVG is embedded as an image (much like a gif). The negatives? It can become quite verbose, and its future is rather unclear (back in 2015, support for SMIL was dropped from Chrome, but this decision was quickly reversed).

The Web Animations API, or WAAPI, is the most modern animation method, has more advanced capabilities than CSS or SMIL, and in general is more flexible and concise. I would recommend it over CSS or SMIL for generative art, but it does have its limitations. It's not suitable for open-ended, exploratory animations, where we're unsure of the end result. Like CSS and SMIL, everything needs to be tightly orchestrated and intentional. To go "full generative," we need something more low level like `requestAnimationFrame()`.

Yes, `requestAnimationFrame()` can make us trudge a rather punishing path to achieve relatively meager results, but conversely, more complicated results can in many cases be achieved in a far more simple and elegant manner than they can using other methods (I'll demonstrate this in our next example on collision detection). We just need to persevere beyond the initial pain barrier.

It's also worth noting that there are many solid third-party libraries out there to help you animate with SVG; of particular note is the GreenSock Animation Platform (GSAP), which is very feature rich and offers robust performance and impressive backward compatibility. It's not open source however, and some of its plug-ins are for paid subscribers only. Anime.js is a nice open source alternative.

# Collision Detection

It's one thing to interact ourselves with a generative piece to influence the output, but it's another thing entirely when it begins to interact with *itself*. This is in essence what collision detection entails. We'll explore an example using the bounds of a rectangle as a basic collision barrier, and we'll utilize the requestAnimationFrame() method while it's still relatively fresh in our minds.

## Setting Boundaries

So the usual drill – create a new folder from the template, rename it to 19-collision-detection, and begin coding below the background. The first thing we'll do is create a rect styled like a picture frame. This effect is achieved by using a slightly transparent stroke over the fill; half the stroke is painted outside the frame and half inside (something we'll need to factor into our collision detection calculations later). The size of this frame will be randomized, so we'll set up a frameSize variable to capture this and also use it to keep other element (like the stroke-width) in proportion.

```
// Create a frame to act as the boundary.
let frameSize = Gen.random(350, 700);
let frame = svg.create('rect').set({
  x: (1000 - frameSize) / 2,
  y: (1000 - frameSize) / 2,
  width: frameSize,
  height: frameSize,
  fill: '#252525',
  stroke: `hsl(${Gen.random(0, 360)} 80% 80% / 0.25)`,
  stroke_width: frameSize / 10,
});
```

# Initializing and Extending Our Shapes

With the frame now in place, let's fill it with some circles of various sizes. The aim will be to have these circles burst out from the center in all directions, some rushing rapidly and others ambling slowly, and all of them bouncing off the frame borders as they encounter them. In the following, we'll start by initializing the circles and filling up an array as we've done in our previous examples.

```
// Randomise the number of circles and set up an empty array.
let numCircles = Math.floor(frameSize / 20);
let circles = [];

// Populate this array.
for (let i = 0; i < numCircles; i += 1) {

  // Randomise the radius relative to the frame size.
  let radius = Gen.random(frameSize / 100, frameSize / 25);

  // Apply the above variables and randomise the hue.
  let circle = svg.create('circle').set({
    cx: 500,
    cy: 500,
    r: radius,
    fill: `hsl(${Gen.random(0, 360)} 80% 80% / 0.5)`
  });

  // Store the circle in the array.
  circles.push(circle);
}
```

We have our circles all clustered in the center now, but they're not yet primed for movement. We have a way to track their position (via the cx and cy attributes), but we have no attributes to track their speed or direction, which we'll need if we're going to pull off collision detection.

Thankfully SvJs elements are easily extendable. If we want to add a new attribute to an element, it's as simple as including it in the set() method. If it's not a valid SVG attribute, it won't have any impact on the rendered SVG, but that's ok – we simply want it stored to be used in our collision detection calculations later.

We'll need at least two new attributes: one to track the speed on the x axis and another to track the speed on the y axis. To determine direction, we can use these same attributes and invert the polarity to change the direction. For example, positive numbers on the x axis will indicate left-to-right motion, and negative numbers will mean right-to-left motion. On the y axis, positive numbers will denote downward motion and negative numbers upward motion.

Setting these new attributes will be a two-step process. We'll first set up variables velocityX and velocityY to capture randomized speeds. And the attributes we'll set will be simply vx and vy, and we'll randomize their polarity using Gen.chance() (so they'll have a 50/50 chance of being either positive or negative). Update the relevant code as follows:

```
// Create variables to control the speed on the x and y axes.
let velocityX = Gen.random(0.1, 5, true);
let velocityY = Gen.random(0.1, 5, true);

// Apply the above variables and randomise the hue.
let circle = svg.create('circle').set({
  cx: 500,
  cy: 500,
  r: radius,
  vx: Gen.chance() ? velocityX : -velocityX,
  vy: Gen.chance() ? velocityY : -velocityY,
  fill: `hsl(${Gen.random(0, 360)} 80% 80% / 0.5)`
});
```

# Frame-by-Frame Calculations

Calculating whether or not one of our circles collides with a boundary (i.e., the edge of our frame) involves keeping a constant check on each circle's position. For this reason, requestAnimationFrame() is really the only feasible way to simulate collision detection, as these checks need to occur on a frame-by-frame basis.

There's a bit of a code dump coming up, but I'll explain the important parts. You'll notice that when we fetch any of our attributes, we're wrapping them in a Number() method. This is because our attributes will be returned as strings, and if we're to do any reliable calculations with them, we want to explicitly handle them as numeric values rather than relying on JavaScript's covert casting (which may sometimes get things right, but it leaves you wide open to bugs).

Here's a rundown of the algorithm we'll implement. First, we calculate the lower and upper bounds (i.e., the frame edges). Then, for each circle:

- We retrieve the position and velocity and store them as variables.

- If the x variable is less than or equal to either the lower bound or the upper bound, we reverse the polarity of the x velocity variable.

- We repeat the previous step for the y axis.

- We then update the x and y variables based on the calculated velocity.

- Finally, we apply the updated variables to the circle element.

Here's the concrete coded version:

```
// Get the lower and upper bounds (the frame edges) for use in
the loop.
let lowerBound = Number(frame.get('x'));
let upperBound = lowerBound + frameSize;

// The animation loop.
function animate() {

  // Check collisions for each circle.
  circles.forEach((circle) => {

    // Retrieve the position and velocity.
    let cx = Number(circle.get('cx'));
    let cy = Number(circle.get('cy'));
    let vx = Number(circle.get('vx'));
    let vy = Number(circle.get('vy'));

    // Check for collisions, and if found reverse the polarity.
    if (cx <= lowerBound || cx >= upperBound) vx = -vx;
    if (cy <= lowerBound || cy >= upperBound) vy = -vy;

    // Update the position.
    cx += vx;
    cy += vy;

    // Set the new values.
    circle.set({ cx: cx, cy: cy, vx: vx, vy: vy });
  });

  // The recursive bit.
  requestAnimationFrame(animate);
}

// Call the animation.
animate();
```

If you watch the animation at this point, you'll notice that the circles do indeed rebound within the vicinity of the frame edge, but it's far from precise and even appears to differ depending on the circle size. Looks like we've left something out of our calculations.

To fix this, we need to account for the fact that the frame border is inset; that is, the stroke is halfway inside the frame, and the radius of each circle is different. This means that the lower bound and upper bound variables must be calculated *inside* the animation loop, as they will vary per circle. There are, however, a couple of static values that can be captured outside the loop and used later inside it: the frame edge and frame inset. Delete the lower bound and upper bound variables and replace them with the following:

```
// Get the frame edge point (x or y) and the inset.
let frameEdge = Number(frame.get('x'));
let frameInset = Number(frame.get('stroke-width')) / 2;
```

Now, inside the loop, we can work out the proper lower bound and upper bound values.

```
// The animation loop.
function animate() {

  // Check collisions for each circle.
  circles.forEach((circle) => {

    // Calculate the lower and upper bounds for each circle.
    let radius = Number(circle.get('r'));
    let lowerBound = frameEdge + radius + frameInset;
    let upperBound = frameEdge + frameSize - radius -
    frameInset;

    // ... remainder of code is unchanged.

}
```

This should result in accurate collision detection; Figure 7-3 shows a freezeframe of this in action. There are a lot of ways you could take this further – add noise into the mix, see if you can incorporate cursor tracking, or change the colors over time. As it is however, we've taken the first steps on the road to full-on physics simulations (a topic way beyond the scope of this book, but I'd encourage you to explore it independently).

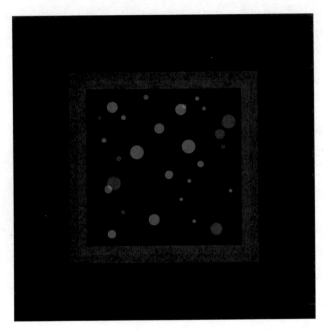

***Figure 7-3.*** *Colorful collision detection*

# Circularity

We'll round off the chapter with a return to the JavaScript Web Animations API. We'll touch on trigonometry in the process, but only tangentially (if you got that pun, you're doing well!), as the main focus will be to provide you with some inspiration, not laden you with complicated math.

Let's create a new example folder called 20-circular-loop, copying our template folder. The aim will be to create a looping animation consisting of circles that are themselves arranged in a circle; these kinds of animations hold high hypnotic potential. We'll start in the usual place below our background, initializing some randomized variables.

```
// Randomise some variables.
let numCircles = Gen.random(20, 35);
let baseRadius = Gen.random(5, 25, true);
let hue = Gen.random(0, 360);
```

We'll use numCircles to control how many times our loop runs and also in the calculations needed to distribute these circles. The baseRadius and hue we'll use as starter values. For now, create the loop and the circles as follows, omitting the cx and cy attributes (which we'll work out in the next section).

```
// Set up the loop.
for (let i = 0; i < numCircles; i += 1) {
  // Create the circle, but don't set the position or
    radius yet.
  let circle = svg.create('circle').set({
    r: baseRadius,
    fill: 'none',
    stroke: `hsl(${hue} 80% 80% / 0.75)`,
    transform_origin: '500 500'
  });

}
```

## Slices of PI

Here comes the trigonometry tangent we mentioned earlier. To calculate the distribution of each of our circles (i.e., their cx and cy coordinates), we need to draw upon some built-in JavaScript Math methods and properties. The first is Math.PI, a property that returns the approximated value of $\pi$ (3.14), a mathematical constant that represents the ratio of a circle's circumference (the length along its perimeter) to its diameter (double the radius). Figure 7-4 illustrates these values.

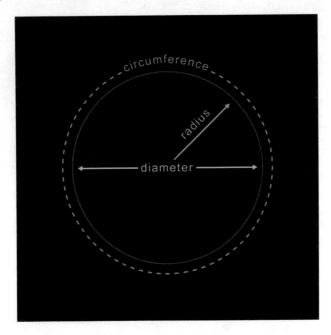

***Figure 7-4.*** *The circumference, diameter, and radius of a circle*

You may be accustomed to angles being expressed in terms of degrees, but in JavaScript, angles are measured in radians by default. One radian is equivalent to the length of a circle's radius wrapped around the circumference (visualized in Figure 7-5). It takes just over six of these radians (or approximately 6.28) to wrap around the full circumference. And half of 6.28 is $\pi$, or 3.14.

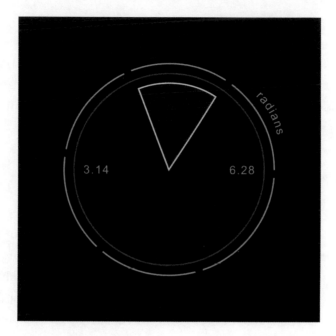

**Figure 7-5.** *How radians relate to π and the circumference*

The takeaway? Math.PI radians is equivalent to 180°, meaning Math.PI * 2 gives us a full circle (360°). So within the context of our loop, we're going to increment the angle at which our circles are placed relative to Math.PI * 2. And to ensure an equal distribution of our circles along the circumference, we'll divide Math.PI * 2 by numCircles, and each time the loop runs, we'll multiply it by our iterator to move on to the next "slice," so to speak.

Within the loop, after we define our circle element, include the following line:

```
// Calculate the current angle.
let angle = Math.PI * 2 / numCircles * i;
```

# Sine and Cosine

Once we have the angle, we need to get the corresponding sine and cosine values, which you can think of as the x and y coordinates. We won't go into too much detail here; suffice to say, the methods `Math.sin()` and `Math.cos()` work together perfectly to create circular motion.

```
// Get the sine and cosine of the angle.
let sin = Math.sin(angle);
let cos = Math.cos(angle);
```

It's also worth noting that these are extremely useful methods in their own right, particularly for motion, due to the smooth, oscillating values they produce. For the current sketch, however, we'll limit ourselves to using these values to position our circles only, not animate them. And to position them, we need to map the sine and cosine values to a more usable range, as they return values between -1 and 1 by default.

We'll position our circles relative to the center of the `viewBox` (so 500 on both the x and y axes) and re-map them so that they span a range of 700. This gives us 150 and 850, that is, -350 and +350 either side of the center.

```
// Map the sine and cosine to the desired range.
let cx = Gen.map(sin, -1, 1, 200, 800, false);
let cy = Gen.map(cos, -1, 1, 200, 800, false);
```

# Animating Our Circles

We can now try our hand at a basic animation. We'll start simple and move our circles outward from the center toward the cx and cy coordinates we defined earlier.

```
// Move from (500, 500) to (cx, cy).
circle.animate({
```

```
  cx: [500, cx, 500],
  cy: [500, cy, 500],
}, {
  duration: 10000,
  iterations: Infinity,
  easing: ['ease-in-out']
});
```

This gets things moving, but it's not an especially interesting sequence. Let's add more variety to it by setting an initial and target radius, using the iterator value to vary these per circle, and rotating the entire animation while we're at it. And just before we close out the loop, let's increment the hue relative to the number of circles to get a nice color distribution.

```
// Set the initial and target radii.
let r1 = baseRadius * 2 + (i * 10);
let r2 = baseRadius / (i + 10);

// Move from (500, 500) to (cx, cy), reduce the radius, rotate.
circle.animate({
  cx: [500, cx, 500],
  cy: [500, cy, 500],
  r: [r1, r2, r1],
  transform: ['rotate(0deg)', 'rotate(360deg)']
}, {
  duration: 10000,
  iterations: Infinity,
  easing: ['ease-in-out']
});

// Increment the hue.
hue = (hue % 360) + (180 / numCircles);
```

There... That gets us much closer to achieving that hypnotic pull. See Figure 7-6 for a snapshot of this animation at about 15% progression.

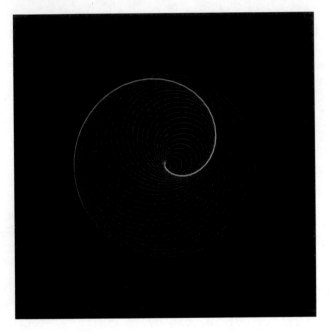

***Figure 7-6.*** *A circular loop with the Web Animations API*

## Summary

This has been perhaps the densest of all chapters so far in terms of concepts and content, but I hope you've also had some fun following along. To quickly recap, we've covered the following:

- Event listeners, event types, and event parameters

- How to save our SVG markup

- How to use cursor tracking to make a sketch interactive

- Animating with CSS keyframes

- Animating with SMIL

- The Web Animations API

- Animating with the requestAnimationFrame() method

- Basic collision detection

- Very basic trigonometry

In the next and final full chapter, we'll focus on SVG filters.

# CHAPTER 8

# Filter Effects

In addition to all the vector functionality offered by SVG (as you'd expect from a format called Scalable Vector Graphics), SVG also provides some very powerful pixel-based effects in the form of the `<filter>` element. Many of the kinds of image-manipulation operations routinely found in editors like GIMP or Photoshop, such as blurs, drop shadows, and distortions, can actually be carried out in SVG too. In this chapter, we'll learn how this is done.

We won't be covering the capabilities of SVG filters in any kind of comprehensive way; that would require at least its own book. It is a vast subject and one whose creative potential – at least aesthetically – is often neglected. It's very easy to make awful-looking SVG filters. I'll aim to avoid this pitfall and will be presenting a subset of filters more from the perspective of the generative artist than the image editor.

## Filter Fundamentals

Before we explore specific filter effects in any depth, we need to know how they're structured. A filter consists of a single `<filter>` element and one or more filter primitives. These primitives, which are also elements, are nested within the main filter element, and they all begin with the letters fe (for filter effect) followed by a descriptive name. Each performs its own operation(s) and can be connected to other primitives in a node-like manner using a series of inputs and outputs.

© David Matthew 2024
D. Matthew, *Generative Art with JavaScript and SVG*, Design Thinking,
https://doi.org/10.1007/979-8-8688-0086-3_8

Let's look at a basic example in raw markup form, using just a single primitive.

```
<svg xmlns="http://www.w3.org/2000/svg" viewBox="0 0
1000 1000">
  <defs>
    <filter id="blur">
      <feGaussianBlur stdDeviation="10" />
    </filter>
  </defs>
  <circle r="350" cx="500" cy="500" fill="yellow"
filter="url(#blur)" />
</svg>
```

As you can see, the `<filter>` element must be nested inside a `<defs>` element; in common with gradients and patterns, it only gets rendered when referenced via a `url` link to its `id`. In the preceding case, a yellow circle calls the filter via its own `filter` attribute, and the result (shown in Figure 8-1) is a soft blur, controlled by a primitive named `feGaussianBlur`.

**Figure 8-1.**  *A blurred circle*

# The Ins and Outs

Let's inspect a slightly more involved example, this time illustrating how filter primitives can be connected together. The result will be a drop shadow applied to a circle's stroke, as shown in Figure 8-2.

```
<svg xmlns="http://www.w3.org/2000/svg" viewBox="0 0
1000 1000">
  <defs>
    <filter id="shadow">
      <feGaussianBlur stdDeviation="25" in="SourceAlpha"
      result="blur" />
      <feOffset dx="0" dy="50" in="blur" result="offset" />
      <feComposite in="SourceGraphic" in2="offset" />
    </filter>
  </defs>
```

```
<circle r="300" cx="500" cy="500" fill="none"
stroke="#475569" stroke-width="50" filter="url(#shadow)" />
</svg>
```

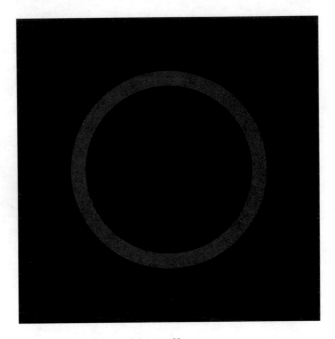

**Figure 8-2.**  *A drop-shadow filter effect*

As with the previous example, we're starting off with an
feGaussianBlur primitive, but you'll notice there's a couple of more
attributes added: in and result. These attributes are also present in the
primitive following it, feOffset. In the final filter primitive, feComposite,
in is also present, along with in2. What do these mean?

- in refers to a filter primitive's input source.

- in2 refers to a second input source, if the filter primitive
  supports this.

- result is what we use to label a filter primitive's output,
  which can then be used as the input for another primitive.

If a filter primitive is the first in its chain (as feGaussianBlur is above), in will default to SourceGraphic; otherwise, it will default to the result of the preceding primitive. SourceGraphic just means the graphics element to which a filter is applied. SourceAlpha also refers to this same graphics element but is restricted to its alpha channel (i.e., its opacity value).

So here's what's happening in this second example:

1.  The feGaussianBlur primitive takes the SourceAlpha of the circle as its input and applies a Gaussian blur effect to it. The result (or output) is then named blur.

2.  The feOffset primitive takes the blur result as its input and offsets it along the y axis, and the result of this is labelled offset.

3.  The feComposite primitive takes our original SourceGraphic as the first input in and the result of offset as its second input in2, recombining them.

We'll go into some of these primitives in more detail later, but next we'll look at how to move from markup to scripting filters with SvJs.

## The SvJs createFilter( ) Method

Perhaps unsurprisingly, SvJs has its own createFilter() method to speed up the filter creation process. It requires just one argument: an id, and this id is used when applying the filter to the target element. As with the createGradient() and createPattern() methods, sensible defaults are initialized, and the checking of whether a defs element already exists is taken care of under the hood.

The following is the SvJs equivalent of our first example shown previously, applying a soft blur to a yellow circle (Figure 8-1).

```
// Initialise the filter.
let filter = svg.createFilter('blur');

// Create the blur effect.
filter.create('feGaussianBlur').set({ stdDeviation: 10 });

// Apply the filter.
svg.create('circle').set({
  r: 350, cx: 500, cy: 500, fill: 'yellow', filter:
'url(#blur)'
});
```

## The Filter Region

When a filter is applied to an element, its active region extends beyond that element. This allows a certain amount of space into which the effect can "bleed," to use a print analogy. This space is known as the filter region, and once a filter's effect extends beyond this region, clipping occurs (see Figure 8-3).

***Figure 8-3.*** *A clipped filter region*

In generative art, we'll sometimes stray outside the range of values a filter effect parameter might anticipate, so it's important to know about this region if your filter effects are unexpectedly clipped. A filter region is defined just as a rect element is: by x, y, width, and height attributes. By default, these values are as follows:

```
<filter x="-10%" y="-10%" width="120%" height="120%">
```

The percentage values are relative to the shape to which the filter is applied, so in the aforementioned, this translates to a 10% padding surrounding the filtered element. SvJs enlarges this filter region to 25%, allowing some more room to experiment. If you need to adjust it further, you can easily do so with the set() method:

```
filter.set({ x: '-15%', y: '-15%', width: '130%', height:
'130%' });
```

# Filter Effects 101

Let's move on to some simple custom filter effects. We've already seen the feGaussianBlur primitive in action so I won't give it its own section here, but it's worth mentioning before I move on that its main attribute stdDeviation can actually accept two values as well as one. If you supply two, the first number will control the blur along the x axis and the second the blur along the y axis.

```
// Create a 'motion' blur effect.
filter.create('feGaussianBlur').set({ stdDeviation: '20 0' });
```

## Shadows

We implemented a drop shadow earlier using three connected filter primitives, but there's actually a much easier way to do this. In a more recent revision of the SVG spec, the primitive feDropShadow was introduced, which can accept up to five attributes: dx, which defines the shadow offset along the x axis; dy, which does the same along the y axis; stdDeviation, which controls the blurring of the shadow; and two more optional attributes, flood-colour and flood-opacity, which can modify the shadow's color and transparency.

Here's how we could rewrite the code for Figure 8-2 using SvJs and the feDropShadow primitive.

```
// Initialise the filter.
let filter = svg.createFilter('shadow');

// Create the drop shadow.
filter.create('feDropShadow').set({ dx: 0, dy: 50,
stdDeviation: 25 });

// Apply the filter.
svg.create('circle').set({
```

```
  // ... other attributes.
  filter: 'url(#shadow)'
});
```

# Coloring

We mentioned earlier some attributes called flood-colour and flood-opacity that can be used with the feDropShadow primitive. There's another primitive these can also be applied to and to which they originally belonged: feFlood. The feFlood primitive is very basic; it requires no input and simply floods the filter region with a specific color and opacity. By itself, it's not especially interesting, but it can be useful when combined with other primitives.

Other more capable color-related primitives exist called feColorMatrix and feComponentTransfer. The latter is too advanced to cover in this book so we'll limit ourselves to feColorMatrix and feFlood. Let's set up a sketch and put these to use.

Instead of copying our template folder, let's copy our first grid example, which I labelled 07-regular-grids (see Chapter 4). Copy and rename this folder to something like 21-colour-filter. Leaving the rest of the code as is, replace the body of the nested for loop with the following:

```
if (Gen.chance(55)) {
  grid.create('rect').set({
    x: x, y: y, width: cellSize, height: cellSize,
    fill: `rgb(
      ${[Gen.random(0, 255), Gen.random(0, 255), Gen.
      random(0, 255)]}
    )`
  });
}
```

This should give us a chance arrangement of colorful tiles on each refresh. So far we've been quite restrained in our use of color, controlling mainly the hue component of the hsl() function. This time we're unleashing the full rgb color spectrum, so the results can range from dramatic and dynamic to garish and grating (see Figure 8-4 for some sample output). There is something I like about these results; the coloring, however, can get a little too incongruous at times. So let's use some filters to rein in the colors but retain the dynamic range.

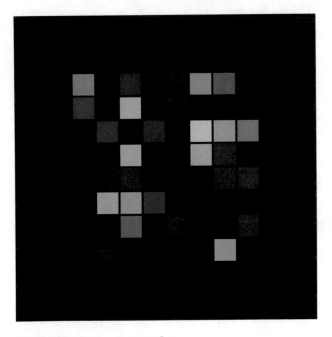

***Figure 8-4.*** *Full-spectrum RGB tiles*

The first step is to desaturate the colors. For this, we can use the feColorMatrix primitive, which takes two arguments: type and values. The accepted values depend on the type, which can be as follows:

- saturate: This determines the color saturation of the input. It accepts values between 0 (no saturation) and 1 (full saturation), though higher values may be accepted by browsers to allow for over-saturation.

- hueRotate: This rotates the hue value by a specified angle, which is set in values. Setting values to 180 for example would invert all the hue values of the input source.

- luminanceToAlpha: This converts the lightness of the input to alpha values and requires no values.

- matrix: This is the most complex and powerful of the feColorMatrix types. It accepts a 5 by 5 color transformation matrix as the values, which matrix-multiplies the pixel component values of the input source. It's a little too advanced to delve into in this chapter.

Of the aforementioned, saturate is what we're looking for. To drain the colors from our input, we need to set the values to 0. Let's set up a filter now to do this. At the bottom of the sketch, initialize a new filter as follows:

```
// Initialise the filter.
let filter = svg.createFilter('colourise');

// De-saturate the input.
filter.create('feColorMatrix').set({
  type: 'saturate',
  values: 0,
  result: 'desaturate'
});

// Apply the filter.
grid.set({ filter: 'url(#colourise)' });
```

This should result in a grayscale grid. Next, we want to choose a color to mix into it, and for this, we'll use the feFlood primitive. Between the feColorMatrix primitive and the last line where we apply the filter, add the following code:

```
// Set a flood colour.
filter.create('feFlood').set({
  flood_color: '#7F462C',
  result: 'flood'
});
```

This should add a sepia-brown color to the composition. The problem? It simply floods the canvas, covering everything else. We need a way to blend it with the result of the feColorMatrix desaturation.

# Blending

Most vector and image editing applications have blending capabilities built in, in the form of layer blending modes. SVG supports this feature at the filter level in the form of the feBlend primitive.

A blending mode (or just blend mode) defines how colors interact when elements overlap (whether the elements are individual shapes or entire layers). If a blend mode is set to multiply for example, the final color is the result of multiplying the top color by the bottom color, which creates an effect similar to transparent film cells overlapping. If set to screen, the top and bottom colors are inverted, multiplied, and re-inverted, resulting in an effect similar to two images shone onto a projection screen.

There are a number of blend modes supported by the SVG spec, and describing each one is beyond the scope of this chapter, but for a comprehensive treatment (including interactive examples), check out the MDN entry at developer.mozilla.org/docs/Web/CSS/blend-mode.

There are actually several blend modes that will work well in our case, so what I'm going to do is store these in an array so we can select from them later. Include the following code before our filter is initialized:

```
// Set up a blend modes array.
let blendModes = ['screen', 'overlay', 'lighten', 'color-
dodge', 'soft-light', 'color'];
```

Next, after where we defined the feFlood primitive, set up the feBlend primitive. We'll randomize its mode attribute and set the first input to the flood color and the second input to the desaturated grid.

```
// Randomise the blend mode.
filter.create('feBlend').set({
  mode: Gen.random(blendModes),
  in: 'flood',
  in2: 'desaturate',
  result: 'blend'
});
```

The first input, in, acts as our top color, and the second input, in2, acts as our background color. Our grid should have re-appeared at this point in colorized form, but we've still got our flood color in the foreground. We need a way to strip this out, which brings us to the next section.

## Compositing

If you've ever watched the behind-the-scenes footage of some of your favorite films, you'll likely have come across the green-screen technique: the action hero who scales a skyscraper is, in reality, hanging from a pulley with green fabric draped in the background. This technique makes it easier to strip away the background from the foreground and combine it later with separately captured footage.

Compositing is the act of fusing these two disparate elements together; two sources combine and become one. It is similar to blending in many respects, but the results are more pronounced and programmable. It has more to do with how elements intersect than how their colors merge, and the various compositing operations available to us can produce very different results. Blending, on the other hand, tends to be more uniform in its output.

The feComposite primitive allows us to perform compositing operations in SVG. It takes two inputs, in and in2, and there are seven possible values its operator attribute accepts: over, in, atop, xor, out, lighter, and arithmetic. In Figure 8-5, I've illustrated six of these; the arithmetic operator has no set output (it's fully customizable) and is a little too complex to properly cover in this chapter.

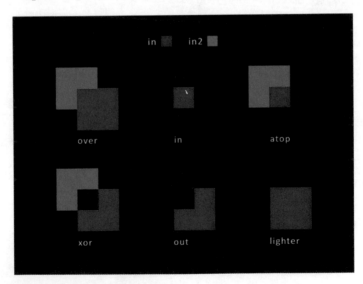

***Figure 8-5.*** *Six of the seven SVG compositing operations*

Because the feComposite primitive is so useful and something you'll likely lean on if you further explore SVG filters, it's worth describing each preset operator. In Figure 8-5, we can think of in as our foreground and in2 as our green-screen background.

- over: This is the default operator, where our foreground is simply placed over the background.

- in: The portion of the foreground that overlaps with the background becomes the new output.

- atop: The portion of the foreground that overlaps with the background is retained; the rest of the foreground is clipped.

- xor: Those portions of the foreground and background that do not overlap are kept; the rest is removed. It's essentially the inverse of the in operator.

- out: The portion of the foreground that falls outside the background is displayed.

- lighter: The overlapping regions of the foreground and background are summed together (resulting in a lightening effect).

- arithmetic: If this operator is chosen, four additional attributes must be defined, all numeric: k1, k2, k3, and k4. The output is then defined via the following formula: (k1 * i1 * i2) + (k2 * i1) + (k3 * i2) + k4, where i1 and i2 represent in and in2, respectively. Yep, told you it was complex! But the most subtle and customizable results can be achieved using this operator, so it is well worth independent exploration.

If we take the result of the feFlood primitive as our first input (the foreground) and the SourceGraphic as the second input, the operator that will achieve the effect we're looking for is atop. To recap, with this operator, those portions of the foreground (feFlood) that overlap with the background (SourceGraphic) are retained; the rest of feFlood should be clipped.

Let's set this up now. Include the following code after the feBlend primitive, before the filter is applied to the grid.

```
// Composite the blend 'atop' the original.
filter.create('feComposite').set({
  in: 'blend',
  in2: 'SourceGraphic',
  operator: 'atop'
});
```

For me, this resulted in the output you see in Figure 8-6. I don't know about you, but I see a pugnacious pup putting up his dukes, à la Scrappy-Doo (though that may well be my pareidolia at work). On each refresh, you'll see something quite different, and while the color tones vary, a common palette can be discerned due to the single feFlood color we're drawing upon. This kind of effect would be quite difficult to achieve without filters.

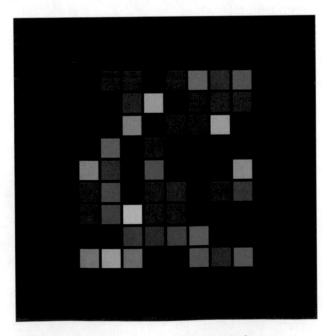

**Figure 8-6.** *The result of the composite operation*

# Noise and Distortion

In this section, we'll introduce a new kind of noise, one that's actually built in to the SVG spec itself. And we'll also explore how to add some distortion to our filter pipeline. With these two ingredients, along with the basics covered earlier, a whole world of effects opens up to us.

## Turbulence

In Chapter 5, we introduced the SvJs `Noise` module, which allowed us to use Perlin noise in our sketches. SVG also implements Perlin noise inside its `feTurbulence` filter primitive, so what's the difference?

Well, with the `Noise` module, we can extract and play with noise *data*, using its values to shape our vectors. With `feTurbulence` on the other hand, we have a filter primitive that renders noise data directly, in *pixel* form. This doesn't give us access to the underlying noise data, but what we can do is easily alter the visual output by tweaking its attributes and then feed it into other filter primitives. The `feTurbulence` attributes are as follows:

- `baseFrequency`: This is the only mandatory attribute, and we can think of it as defining the noise "zoom level." It's typical for the lowest value to start at 0.0001 (though you can start lower), and the higher the values go, the more of our noise terrain is revealed. If you supply two numeric values instead of one, the first will define the frequency along the x axis and the second along the y axis. Decoupling the values this way makes it possible to stretch or compress the resulting texture horizontally or vertically.

- numOctaves: This attribute refers to the number of octaves present in the noise signal and determines the level of detail we can discern. Higher values render more natural results but are more processor-intensive. The most usable results lie in the range of 1 to 5.

- seed: This allows us to change the "location" from which we sample our noise. If the baseFrequency is our zoom level, the seed is our position. A valid seed value should be a positive integer anywhere from 0 to 10 million.

- stitchTiles: This attribute accepts either stitch or noStitch and refers to how adjacent areas of the noise terrain are blended together. With it set to noStitch (the default), certain noise configurations can lead to a "tiling" effect, where the boundary between noise regions is quite pronounced. Setting a value of stitch can soften this.

- type: This can be set to fractalNoise or turbulence (the default). The former produces the same kind of noise pattern across the red, green, blue, and alpha channels, and the latter produces a different pattern in the alpha channel. The fractalNoise type has a softer look and is great for generating gaseous textures like clouds. The turbulence type, on the other hand, is more liquid-like in appearance.

In Figure 8-7, we can see two instances of turbulence on the left and two instances of fractalNoise on the right. The values vary only slightly between instances, which should give you a sense of the potential variation offered by this filter primitive.

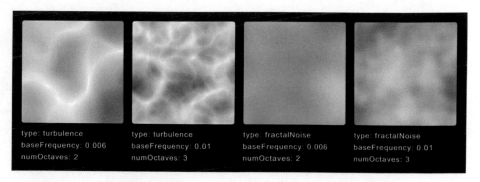

**Figure 8-7.** *Varying the base frequency and octaves for the two noise types*

The best way to get a feel for how feTurbulence works is to tweak an interactive example, so I've created a pen for you here for this purpose: davidmatthew.ie/generative-art-javascript-svg#turbulence. I prefer working with baseFrequency values at the very low end of spectrum and modifying the seed to select a pattern at random; this can produce a huge variety of interesting textures. Very high baseFrequency values can be useful however if you want to simulate something more granular, like the classic film grain effect or a sandpaper-like texture.

# Displacement

One filter primitive that works particularly well alongside feTurbulence is feDisplacementMap. This primitive allows us to distort the first input, in, using values from the second input, in2. This second input acts as the map from which we can derive the displacement values, that is, the values that decide how much distortion we should apply along the x and y axes. This means that we could use the output from feTurbulence to distort our SourceGraphic by feeding both through feDisplacementMap.

Besides the aforementioned in and in2, the feDisplacementMap primitive has three other attributes: the first is scale, which determines how much distortion to apply (i.e., to what extent is in distorted by in2).

The other two attributes, xChannelSelector and yChannelSelector, allow us to specify which channels are responsible for horizontal and vertical displacement. They accept values of R, G, B, or A, representing the three color channels along with the alpha channel.

If we take a single color channel, R, as an example, its value can range from 0 to 255. Values below 127 result in negative displacement (they're shifted left along the x axis, or up along the y axis), whereas values above 127 result in positive displacement (shifted to the right along the x axis, or down along the y axis).

In Figure 8-8, the output of an feTurbulence primitive (center) is used as the map to displace the source graphic (left), resulting in some soft wave-like distortion (right).

***Figure 8-8.*** *Using turbulence as a displacement map source*

## Creating a Cosmic Bubble

This next example will piece together several of the filter primitives we've covered so far and apply it to the simplest of source graphics: the circle. Our aim will be to create something a little "cosmic" by compositing together some turbulence, blur, and distortion.

First things first, make a copy of our template folder and rename it to 22-hubble-bubble (or another name of your choice). In the usual spot below the background, let's set up our source graphic in the center of the viewBox, randomizing its radius a little.

```
// Create the source graphic.
svg.create('circle').set({
  cx: 500,
  cy: 500,
  r: Gen.random(250, 350),
  fill: '#000',
  filter: 'url(#cosmic)'
});
```

You'll notice we've referenced our filter already but haven't yet created it. Normally the order of our created elements matters; if we create one circle and then another, the latter will be rendered "above" the former in a layer-like manner. But as filters are created within a defs element, it's ok to define them after the element to which they apply. To recap, anything that lives inside the defs element isn't directly rendered but must be referenced.

In the next step, we'll create the filter (ensuring the id matches the reference to #cosmic), and add the first filter primitive to the chain: feTurbulence. We'll randomize the seed, keep the dial low on the baseFrequency, and crank up the numOctaves to 4, to bring out some of the texture details.

```
// Initialise the filter.
let filter = svg.createFilter('cosmic');

// Create a random amount of turbulence.
filter.create('feTurbulence').set({
  type: 'fractalNoise',
  baseFrequency: Gen.random(0.002, 0.006, true),
  seed: Gen.random(0, 10000),
  numOctaves: 4,
  stitchTiles: 'stitch',
  result: 'turbulence'
});
```

Like feFlood, feTurbulence is a generator primitive that doesn't require any input; it generates its own output directly. The result of this is that once we initialize an feTurbulence primitive as the latest (or only) link in the filter chain, it will simply flood the filter region with its output (which is what you'll see if you run the code at this point). We'll use feComposite to fix this later.

In our next step, we'll create a target region to displace (i.e., apply distortion to). To create this target area, what we'll do is soften the edges of the source graphic (the circle) using an feGaussianBlur; this has the effect of introducing some transparency to the circle's perimeter. This area of receding transparency (another way of describing a blur) will be what we use to apply distortion to our turbulence. Figure 8-8 shows the result of using turbulence as a displacement map source; this time around we'll be doing the reverse and using turbulence as the displacement map destination. The blurred area of our circle will instead be our displacement map source. Here's how to set up this up (with some randomness mixed in).

```
// Blur the edges of the source graphic.
filter.create('feGaussianBlur').set({
  stdDeviation: Gen.random(10, 25), in: 'SourceGraphic',
  result: 'blurred'
});
```

```
// Displace the turbulence with the blurred edge of the circle.
filter.create('feDisplacementMap').set({
  in: 'turbulence',
  in2: 'blurred',
  scale: Gen.random(250, 500),
  result: 'distortion'
});
```

This results in a rim of displaced noise, as shown in Figure 8-9. Note that we've omitted the xChannelSelector and yChannelSelector attributes of feDisplacementMap; these both default to the alpha channel, which is fine in our case.

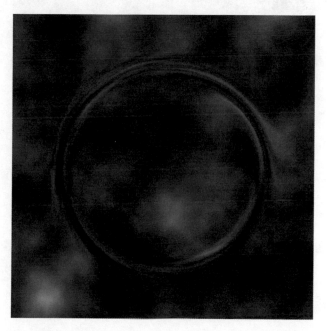

***Figure 8-9.***  *Displacement using the blurred edge of a circle*

We're not fully done yet; as a final step, I want to cut away everything beyond the perimeter of the blurred region. The solution to this is to composite together the outputs of feDisplacementMap and feGaussianBlur using the atop operator. We should then have something that resembles Figure 8-10, our Hubble Bubble.

```
// Remove everything beyond the blurred perimeter.
filter.create('feComposite').set({
  in: 'distortion',
  in2: 'blurred',
  operator: 'atop'
});
```

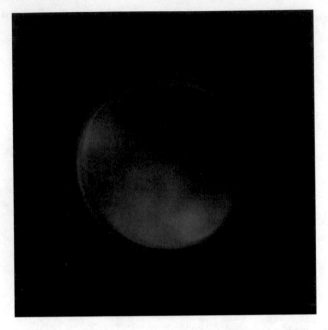

*Figure 8-10.* *One possible iteration of the Hubble Bubble sketch*

# Lighting and Texture

Despite SVG being, by definition, a format for two-dimensional vector graphics, among its filter primitives, you'll find two lighting effects: feDiffuseLighting and feSpecularLighting. Normally the domain of three-dimensional graphics, lighting typically requires a z-axis component to operate so that surfaces or other objects that protrude in space, that is, have depth, can catch the light cast by the source. SVG coordinate space is devoid of any such third dimension or z axis, so how exactly does lighting function in such an environment?

The answer is that the z axis is simulated by using "bump" maps. Specifically, feDiffuseLighting and feSpecularLighting both interpret the alpha channel of their connected inputs as a bump map source. A bump map is just what it sounds like, a map of bumps, meaning any raised regions of a surface, like slopes, peaks, folds, and wrinkles.

The challenge with these lighting primitives is knowing how to supply them with nicely gradiented bump maps; anything with very sharp transitions or a lot of areas of flat color can often appear unpleasantly pixelated, or entirely unaffected. In Figure 8-11, we can see the rather stark difference between a distant light source shining on a circle with a radial gradient (left) vs. a circle of the same size with a uniform fill (right).

***Figure 8-11.*** *Lighting cast on a radial gradient vs. a flat fill*

Lighting is one of those things in SVG that's very easy to get wrong. When it does go awry, the results often look cheap, choppy, and jagged and can put you off playing with lighting altogether. We need to remember that with filters, we've moved from the realm of vectors to that of pixels, where resolution matters. A more finely gradiented alpha channel will translate to a higher-resolution bump map.

Fortunately, feTurbulence is a first-rate source of gradiented alpha channel data. In our next sketch, we'll use feTurbulence along with feDiffuseLighting and feDisplacementMap to simulate a rough, ripped paper effect. But first, we need to delve a little more into the details of the two aforementioned lighting primitives.

# Diffuse and Specular Lighting

The feDiffuseLighting primitive simulates diffuse reflection. What this means is that the light that strikes the surface of a diffuse-lit object is scattered in all directions, as is characteristic of rough surface textures (like linen). The feSpecularLighting primitive, on the other hand, simulates specular reflection, which is characteristic of smoother surfaces (like a bowling ball). With specular reflection, the light that strikes the surface bounces at a definite angle. Figure 8-12 shows the difference between a point light emitted by feDiffuseLighting (left) vs. the same light emitted by feSpecularLighting (right).

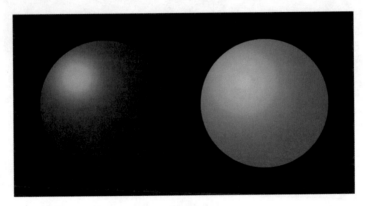

***Figure 8-12.*** *Diffuse vs. specular lighting*

Both lighting primitives take a single input in as their bump map source and a surfaceScale attribute, which defines the relative height of the bump map. The color of the light can also be customized using the lighting-color attribute, which is white by default. Both primitives also share an attribute that defines a constant, diffuseConstant in the case of feDiffuseLighting and specularConstant in the case of feSpecularLighting. This constant determines the strength of the light cast by the source. The feSpecularLighting primitive boasts an additional attribute called `specularExponent`, which controls the focal point strength (in Figure 8-12, this would determine the size of the point light's reflection).

# Light Sources

I've mentioned distant lights and point lights a couple of times now but haven't explained them. These refer to the type of light emitted by either an `feDiffuseLighting` or `feSpecularLighting` primitive. By themselves, these primitives do not emit any light; they require an extra nested node to define the source. In other words, setting up a light in SVG involves defining two elements: one, the outer node, which defines whether the target surface of the lighting is diffuse or specular; and two, the inner node, which defines the type of light source to be used. Here's how an example might look in raw SVG:

```
<feDiffuseLighting in="SourceGraphic" surfaceScale="1.5">
  <feDistantLight azimuth="330" elevation="45" />
</feDiffuseLighting>
```

There are three light source nodes: `feDistantLight`, an ambient light that emits rays uniformly in all directions (such as the sun); `fePointLight`, a more proximate light source that has a defined focal point; and `feSpotLight`, a directional light that emits its rays through a conical shape, the dimensions of which can be customized. Addressing all three light sources would exceed the scope of this chapter, so we'll stick to the first two: `feDistantLight` and `fePointLight`.

The `feDistantLight` source has two attributes: the `azimuth`, which specifies the angle of direction of the light, and the `elevation`, which specifies the height of the light source. Both are expressed in terms of degrees. To use the sun analogy, at dawn it would rise in the east (at an `azimuth` and `elevation` of 0) and by midday at the equator, it would have climbed to an `elevation` of 90, directly overhead.

The fePointLight source has no azimuth or elevation; it is instead defined entirely by x, y, and z attributes. The z attribute would correspond with the elevation or height of the light source, and the x and y attributes refer to the standard two-dimensional position in the current coordinate space.

# Simulating Textures

Let's start a new sketch and flesh out some of the theory mentioned previously. Copy our template folder and rename it to 23-rough-paper, and in the usual spot below the background, create a parchment-colored gradient that we'll apply to our paper. The paper itself will be a compound path consisting of two shapes (the result of ripping it in two). As you can see, it's possible to extend paths beyond a terminating Z command by simply adding a new M command (the equivalent of lifting your pen to start a new line elsewhere). Once we have the ripped paper set up, we center it.

```
// Create a parchment-coloured gradient.
svg.createGradient('parchment', 'linear', ['#fffbeb',
'#fde68a'], 90);

// Create the path for the ripped paper.
let paper = svg.create('path').set({
  fill: 'url(#parchment)',
  stroke: '#4444',
  d: 'M 0,0 h 175 l 175,550 h -350 Z M 210,0 h 340 v
  550 h -165 Z',
  filter: 'url(#rough-paper)'
});

// Centre it.
paper.moveTo(500, 500);
```

The composition we're keeping deliberately simple so that we can give more focus to the filter effect. We'll initialize this next and add the first primitive to the chain: feTurbulence. This will form the basis of the paper grain texture.

```
// Initialise the filter.
let filter = svg.createFilter('rough-paper');

// Add turbulence to simulate paper grain.
filter.create('feTurbulence').set({
  type: 'fractalNoise',
  numOctaves: 5,
  baseFrequency: 0.04,
  seed: Gen.random(0, 100),
  result: 'turbulence'
});
```

The canvas should now be flooded with feTurbulence. What we'll do next is shine a light on it, specifically an feDiffuseLighting primitive with a nested feDistantLight node as the lighting type. This second node we can create directly after the diffuse lighting primitive, using SvJs method chaining.

```
// Shine diffuse lighting on the turbulence.
filter.create('feDiffuseLighting').set({
  surfaceScale: 1,
  diffuseConstant: 1.3,
  in: 'turbulence',
  result: 'lighting'
}).create('feDistantLight').set({
  azimuth: 180,
  elevation: 45,
});
```

We should now have a paper-like texture covering the canvas. Next, we'll rough up the edges of our source graphic by plugging some turbulence into an `feDisplacementMap` primitive.

```
// Distort the paper source graphic with turbulence.
filter.create('feDisplacementMap').set({
  in: 'SourceGraphic',
  in2: 'turbulence',
  scale: 25,
  result: 'distortion'
});
```

This gives us an outline of aging paper with worn edges, but with no texture. To re-introduce the result of the lighting effect, we need to do some compositing. With the lighting output as the foreground and rough-edged paper as the background, the in operator will achieve the effect we're looking for.

```
// Merge the lighting with the rough-edged paper.
filter.create('feComposite').set({
  in: 'lighting',
  in2: 'distortion',
  operator: 'in',
  result: 'composite'
});
```

With the shape now in place and the texture showing through, we have a believable rough and ripped paper texture. However, we're missing one final ingredient: the color. To remedy this, we'll blend the output of `feComposite` with the output of `feDisplacementMap` and use a mode of `multiply`. This should salvage our original parchment gradient.

```
// Re-introduce the parchment gradient.
filter.create('feBlend').set({
```

```
  in: 'composite',
  in2: 'distortion',
  mode: 'multiply'
});
```

Figure 8-13 shows the result. Not bad! While not quite impressive enough to stand on its own (in my opinion at least), with variations of this effect, you have a means of injecting additional visual interest into other generative compositions.

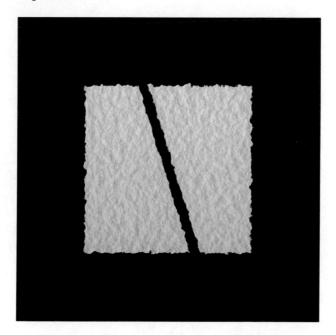

***Figure 8-13.*** *Our rough and ready paper texture*

# Generative Textures

The previous example lays the groundwork for what we'll try next. Simulating textures is all well and good, but for the next example, we'll go full generative, that is, relinquish some control and relish the randomness of the results. In the process, we'll also demonstrate the use of specular lighting of the point variety, so you can see how it differs from diffuse, distant lighting.

Copy the template folder and call it `24-rocky-randomness`. Below the background, we'll set up our source graphic, which will be a simple circle. To this circle, we'll apply both a gradient and a filter.

```
// Create our source graphic.
svg.create('circle').set({
  r: 300,
  cx: 500,
  cy: 500,
  fill: 'url(#random-gradient)',
  filter: 'url(#rocky-randomness)'
});
```

The next step is to set up a linear gradient. For this, we'll use an array of three random colors, and we'll also randomize the gradient's rotation.

```
// A random colour array.
let colours = [
  `hsl(${Gen.random(0, 360)} 80% 80% / 0.75)`,
  `hsl(${Gen.random(0, 360)} 80% 80% / 0.75)`,
  `hsl(${Gen.random(0, 360)} 80% 80% / 0.75)`
];

// A gradient with a randomised rotation and array of colours.
svg.createGradient('random-gradient', 'linear', colours, Gen.
random(0, 360));
```

Now to the filter. As with our other examples, our first node will be an feTurbulence primitive, which will act as our primary textural source. The numOctaves will vary between 2 and 7, which will allow for quite a degree of variation in the level of detail. The baseFrequency and seed we'll also randomize.

236

```
// Initalise the filter.
let filter = svg.createFilter('rocky-randomness');

// Create the primary turbulence.
filter.create('feTurbulence').set({
  type: 'turbulence',
  numOctaves: Gen.random(2, 7),
  baseFrequency: Gen.random(0.003, 0.01, true),
  seed: Gen.random(0, 1000),
  result: 'turbulence'
});
```

Now we have raw turbulence covering the canvas, and while it does vary on each refresh, it still feels a little too uniform. How can we create something more organic and a little less grid-like? Well, we could distort it with ... more turbulence!

To do this, we'll set up another feTurbulence primitive, this time using fractalNoise. The baseFrequency we'll ramp up a little, but we'll keep numOctaves and the seed to a similar range. Then we'll plug both into feDisplacementMap, randomize the scale value (which determines the strength of the distortion), and set R and G as the x and y channel selectors (purely because I didn't really like the default output of alpha on this occasion).

```
// Set up another instance of turbulence.
filter.create('feTurbulence').set({
  type: 'fractalNoise',
  numOctaves: Gen.random(3, 7),
  baseFrequency: Gen.random(0.01, 0.07, true),
  seed: Gen.random(0, 1000),
  result: 'noise'
});
```

```
// Distort the first instance of turbulence with the second.
filter.create('feDisplacementMap').set({
  in: 'turbulence',
  in2: 'noise',
  scale: Gen.random(25, 40),
  xChannelSelector: 'R',
  yChannelSelector: 'G',
  result: 'distortion'
});
```

We have some more natural-looking noise now, so let's spin up some specular lighting and see how the noise looks when lit up. We'll utilize Gen. random() on most of the attributes, including the point light coordinates.

```
// Shine a specular point light on the distorted output.
filter.create('feSpecularLighting').set({
  in: 'distortion',
  surfaceScale: Gen.random(5, 30),
  specularConstant: Gen.random(2, 6),
  specularExponent: Gen.random(10, 25),
  result: 'lighting'
}).create('fePointLight').set({
  x: Gen.random([-50, 500, 1050]),
  y: Gen.random([-50, 1050]),
  z: Gen.random(50, 250)
});
```

For the x and y coordinates, you'll notice we're using Gen.random() to pick from an array of values rather than a range; if you inspect these values, you'll see that these combinations keep the lighting to the periphery of the canvas. This is mainly to prevent any direct shine (think of an unwelcome camera flash in a photograph). If you load up the sketch at this point, you should see some interesting generative terrain emerge. We're not done yet though.

Before we bring the terrain and the source graphic back together, we're going to soften the edges of the latter with some feGaussianBlur. We'll then use feComposite along with the in operator as we've done in previous sketches, before recovering the original gradient using another feComposite primitive, this time with the atop operator.

```
// Blur the source graphic.
filter.create('feGaussianBlur').set({
  in: 'SourceGraphic',
  stdDeviation: Gen.random(25, 50),
  result: 'blur'
});

// Bring the lit texture in via the blurred source graphic.
filter.create('feComposite').set({
  in: 'lighting',
  in2: 'blur',
  operator: 'in',
  result: 'comp1'
});

// Recover the original gradient.
filter.create('feComposite').set({
  in: 'blur',
  in2: 'comp1',
  operator: 'atop'
});
```

And now we're ready to see some results! Figure 8-14 shows a render I particularly liked, but the variation in this sketch is quite large so it's best to play around until you land on something you like.

***Figure 8-14.*** *Specular random rockiness*

And that concludes our foray into filters. As I mentioned before, there's so much more to explore where filters are concerned, and there are quite a few primitives I didn't have the space to touch on. It definitely warrants (and rewards) further independent exploration.

## Summary

Let's do a quick recap of what was covered in this our penultimate chapter:

- How filters are constructed

- Filter regions and the SvJs `createFilter()` method

- Basic primitives like `feGaussianBlur`, `feFlood`, and `feDropShadow`

- More complex primitives like `feComposite` and `feBlend` that tie other primitives together

- The power of the `feTurbulence` primitive and its creative possibilities

- Distorting other primitives using `feDisplacementMap`

- Lighting and how three dimensions can be simulated using bump maps

- Diffuse and specular lighting and the various light source types

- How turbulence, displacement, and lighting can be used together to simulate and generate textures

In the next chapter, we'll wrap things up and touch on some topics that can help take your generative art to the next level.

# CHAPTER 9

# The Generative Way

Congratulations for having come this far! We've covered a lot, so it's time to take stock, stretch out those mental muscles, and make sure we don't end this book with an injury. We'll wind down by reviewing each chapter in little chunks, and we'll wrap up by previewing some of the paths you might pursue next in your generative journey.

## The Journey So Far

We began with an introduction to SVG and what sets it apart from raster formats like PNG and JPG. We then moved on to the SvJs library and learned how to set up a local front-end development environment. The first chapter closed with a bit of a code dump to serve up some visual inspiration, but it was a little light on explanation, so the following two chapters picked up the slack.

For those new to JavaScript and/or programming in general, Chapter 2 offered a primer, while Chapter 3 delved into the core functionality of the SvJs library. We explored how to create basic shapes and how to work with text, groups, gradients, and patterns, and we created some colorful compositions and optical illusions along the way.

With the introduction of randomness in Chapter 4, we were finally able to go full generative and create sketches with results not rigidly set in advance. We learned how to randomize numbers within a range, randomly select items from an array, and construct regular grids using that

© David Matthew 2024
D. Matthew, *Generative Art with JavaScript and SVG*, Design Thinking,
https://doi.org/10.1007/979-8-8688-0086-3_9

staple of generative art, the nested for loop. We extended our knowledge of SVG with masks and clip paths and played with Gaussian and Pareto probability distributions.

Noise was introduced in Chapter 5 as a way of injecting a more organic kind of variation into our sketches, and other useful generative functions were covered to help us constrain and map these noise values to more useful ranges. In Chapter 6, we tapped into the power of the path element and its arsenal of commands, and we learned how to create lines and curves of the quadratic, cubic Bezier, and elliptical arc variety.

Chapter 7 was all about making things move. We explored event listeners and user interaction and reviewed no less than four different ways of animating SVG. We covered basic collision detection and circular motion, before continuing on to filters in Chapter 8. There we focused on a subset of filter primitives of most immediate use to the generative artist, and we learned how to connect these primitives together to achieve a variety of different effects.

# The Voyage Forward

So where do you go from here? Have we fully explored the field of generative art, mapped all the territory? Not in the slightest! We've only really circled the tip of the proverbial iceberg, hinting at the hulking structure beneath. So if you do want to dive a little deeper yourself, I'll tentatively suggest some further topics (with the caveat that the material we've covered so far could be expanded upon ad infinitum).

# Trigonometry

I was only able to offer a very cursory treatment of trigonometry in Chapter 7, so if this was your first time encountering the likes of `Math.PI` and `Math.sin()`, don't expect these concepts to take root (squared or otherwise … apologies, poor pun). Trigonometry is a topic that deserves a deep dive of its own, and like much of the material in this book, the more exposure and practice you get – or better yet, the more you play – the more comfortable you'll be.

That said, I do find that interactive visualizations are a great way to kickstart comprehension, so to that end, I've set up a sketch showing the relationship between circular motion and right-angled triangles (the very foundation of trigonometry), a freezeframe of which you can see in Figure 9-1.

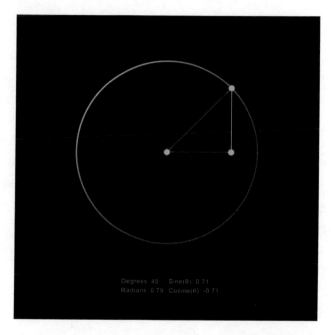

*Figure 9-1.*  *An interactive trigonometry visualization*

As with the rest of the examples in this chapter, it's intended to illustrate rather than instruct, so the code isn't included here. You can, however, play with this particular example on the book's dedicated web page and inspect the code there if so inclined. I've also included further reading and resources that should help you delve into the topic, including those I've relied upon myself over the years. These can be found at `davidmatthew.ie/generative-art-javascript-svg/#trigonometry`.

If you don't consider yourself to be of a particularly mathematical mindset, please don't be dissuaded from exploring this fascinating subject. You only need to be acquainted with a relatively small `subset` of it to tap into its creative possibilities, and this doesn't have to involve complicated equations.

# Fractals

Another subject that doesn't necessitate complicated equations or mind-bending mathematical prowess is fractals. Yes, a fractal is a mathematical object, and some are enormously complex, but fractals in general are based on simple principles of recursion and self-similarity.

Recursion essentially means self-reference. A recursive function is one that continuously calls itself, an example of which we encountered in Chapter 7 with `requestAnimationFrame()`. Self-similarity, in relation to fractals, means that one part will resemble the whole, and vice versa. This is illustrated in Figure 9-2, which shows a famous fractal known as the Sierpinski triangle. As you can see, each building block is a reflection of the structure taken in its entirety.

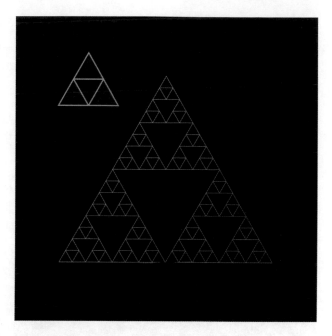

***Figure 9-2.*** *Self-similarity in the Sierpinski triangle*

Where does recursion come in? Well, it can be found in every fractal, including the Sierpinski triangle, but to really illustrate the idea, let's take another well-known specimen, the Von Koch snowflake. The algorithm used to construct this fractal could be distilled down to the following (albeit simplified) steps:

1.    Construct an equilateral triangle.

2.    Divide each side into three segments.

3.    Remove the central segment.

4.    Repeat step 1.

The fourth step is what makes this algorithm recursive. Figure 9-3 shows what this process would look like after just three further iterations. In theory, these steps could continue on indefinitely, producing an ever-more intricate, endlessly magnifiable perimeter, which is why fractals are sometimes seen as "windows into infinity." In practice, iterations are usually limited in line with screen resolution or otherwise capped to prevent our browsers crashing and our processors crunching numbers they can no longer handle.

***Figure 9-3.*** *Recursively constructing the Von Koch snowflake*

Fractals open up an entire universe of exploration and inspiration for the generative artist, far beyond what I've been able to hint at here. If your interest is piqued at this point, I've pooled together further resources at davidmatthew.ie/generative-art-javascript-svg/#fractals that I'd encourage you to explore.

# Systems Simulations

From simple rules, unexpected complexity often emerges; this is not only true for fractals, but for a number of natural systems. Simulating such systems is usually the business of serious science, but in the more advanced areas of generative art, you'll see simulations of basic physics (think gravity, mass, density, etc.), particle systems (like fog, fire, and smoke), and organic behavior (from single cell interactions to the flocking patterns of birds).

Now, SVG isn't always the medium of choice for systems simulations – particle systems, for example, will perform better in pixel-based environments like the HTML canvas – but performance concerns aside, if you're looking to add an extra layer to your compositions, sprinkling a bit of science on top of the art, simulating natural systems can certainly be worth the work involved. A single sketch could become the basis of an endless stream of creative output, as much application as artwork.

John Conway's Game of Life is a good example of an organic simulation; it's a grid-based, zero-player game that simulates patterns of growth, decline, and evolution. Each cell in the grid can be in one of two states: "alive" or "dead." Living cells contain a fill color; dead cells do not. The rules that underpin the game are surprisingly simple, yet complexity can nonetheless emerge in the form of unexpected patterns and clusters of cells battling it out for survival. These rules are as follows:

1.  Any living cell with either one or zero neighbors dies.

2.  Any living cell with either two or three neighbors survives to the next "generation" (or iteration).

3.  Any living cell with four or more neighbors dies.

4.  Any empty (i.e., dead) cell with exactly three neighbors spawns to life.

Figure 9-4 shows a game a few generations in. Some clusters (like the square of cells in the top left and bottom right corners) are in stasis, meaning they survive but don't spread and thrive. Other cells are actively sprawling, exploring, disappearing, and re-spawning. It can be fun to watch!

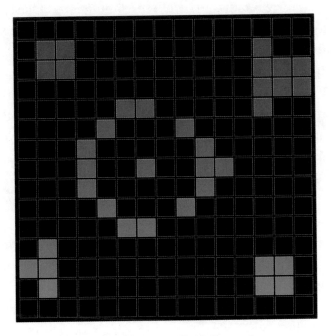

***Figure 9-4.*** *A snapshot of a Game of Life in action*

I'll link to more examples for you to play with at davidmatthew.ie/ generative-art-javascript-svg/#systems-simulations, including other kinds of simulations.

# Closing Comments

At this stage, I've done enough summarizing, so I'd like to leave you with some (rather opinionated) parting tips to support you in your generative endeavors:

- Be comfortable never knowing enough. With any kind of coding, there's always so much more to know. And that's ok.

- Try to block off bits of time to play with code; you don't need to commit to all-nighters. Small habit-forming steps are more sustainable than the odd sprint here and there.

- Embrace simplicity; generative art doesn't have to be complicated to be good.

- Take inspiration from other artists; reverse-engineer examples that inspire you.

- Don't just copy; understand what you implement, and always put your own spin on things. It'll help you develop your own style.

- Give back. Get involved in the community. Contribute code, constructive critiques, or simply leave a positive comment on another artist's work and let them know you appreciate their efforts.

- And finally, appreciate your own efforts, regardless of the results. Output isn't everything, and your generative journey is your own.

# Index

## A

A (or a) command, 150
addEventListener(), 168
animate() function, 185, 187
Automatism, 86

## B

Bitmap images, 2

## C

callback functions, 47, 168–171
C command, 156
Circularity
    animating circles, 200–202
    PI slices, 198, 199
    randomized variables, 197
    sine/cosine, 200
Collision detection
    frame-by-frame
        calculations, 193–196
    initializing/extending shapes,
        191, 192
    setting boundaries, 190
Comparison operators, 29
Conditional statements, 31–33, 53

createCurve() method, 163
createGradient() method, 76, 77
createPattern() method, 209
Cubic Bezier curve
    control point coordinates,
        156, 157
    organic curves, 159, 160,
        162, 163
    symmetry, 158
    varying curve factor, 165

## D

defs element, 75, 77–79, 209, 225

## E

Elliptical arcs
    arguments, 150
    generative arcs, 153, 155, 156
    irregular radii, 152
    setting flags, 151, 152
Event listeners
    cursor tracking, creating, 171–173
    event types, 168, 169
    JavaScript programmers, 167
    parameters, 169
    SvJs save method, 170, 171

© David Matthew 2024
D. Matthew, *Generative Art with JavaScript and SVG*, Design Thinking,
https://doi.org/10.1007/979-8-8688-0086-3

Printed in the United States
by Baker & Taylor Publisher Services